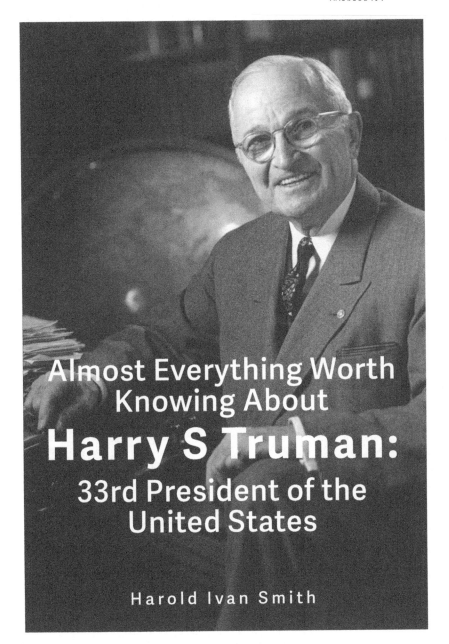

Almost Everything Worth Knowing About
Harry S Truman:
33rd President of the United States

Harold Ivan Smith

ISBN: 978-0-578-64668-8
Printed in the United States of America

Design by Jack Martin
Cover photo: Portrait of Harry S. Truman,
September 1958, used with permission of
Harry S. Truman Presidential Library
Back cover photo: Public domain

Dedication

Research on the life of America's 33rd president is possible because of two institutions' intense dedication to preserving and enhancing the legacy of Harry S Truman.

Through their stewardship of their resources they open the door to curiosity, historical knowledge, and even amazement by scholars and ordinary citizens. Their boards, administrators, staffs, volunteers, and generous supporters make it possible for researchers, historians, biographers, and writers like me to explore ideas, concepts, and hunches.

Just as the world is a better place because of Harry S and Bess Truman, the world is a better place because of two institutions.

With gratitude I dedicate this book to

The Harry Truman Presidential Library
Independence, Missouri

The Truman Library Foundation
Kansas City, Missouri

Contents

Foreword vi

Preface vii

Acknowledgments..x

Introduction... xii

Childhood..13

Young Adult 18

Soldier 23

Family 28

Harry, Bess, and Margaret 33

County Judge 46

U.S. Senator..52

Vice President..61

Early Presidency 67

World War II..75

President..84

Defining Global Responsibility.......................................102

Recognizing the State of Israel.......................................107

Election of 1948 113

Turmoil in China and Korea..128

Civil Rights...144

McCarthyism 153

Critics 158

Observations and Assessments 163

Independence, Missouri..172

Religion 178

Post-Presidency 187

Harry "Being Harry"...199

Truman on His Contemporaries 213

Christmas 219

Money 224

End of Life..230

Legacy 235

Conclusion 244

Sources 245

About the Author..261

Foreword

True to its title, this book covers a wide range of information about our 33rd president and presents it in an unconventional format—arranged in the form of multiple-choice exam—but without a grader. Since correct answers appear with each chronological section, the reader may satisfy her curiosity by looking at them in whatever sequence he chooses. In that sense, he will test himself. With all the sources that the author quotes, Harold Ivan Smith has obviously researched widely in the historical and biographical literature.

One may also note that there is Truman trivia here, but also statements that have worldwide significance because of the import of Truman's policies in a decade that shaped the world after the cataclysm of World War II. One may also draw conclusions about the character, knowledge, and experience that our 33rd president brought to his leadership in the critical period of our history. The reader can begin to see why Harry S Truman has been rated fifth or sixth among our best presidents according to American historians and political scientists polled since President Truman's death in December 1972.

This book is an interesting and challenging way to add to the store of knowledge about a president who set an example for all of his successors in the Oval Office, whether they abide by it or not. It is to America's detriment when our presidents ignore or defy such examples from the past. As President Truman liked to tell young people, "Study your history, find out how you got this republic, and learn what it takes to keep it."

—Niel M. Johnson, PhD, author,
Power, Money, and Women: Words to the Wise
from Harry S Truman

Preface

A word to readers about methodology and interpretation:

Here are some suggestions for getting the most out of this book.

Read each question carefully. A question may contain a clue that narrows the potential answer(s) from the four choices offered. Be aware that some questions have more than one correct answer.

Remember that the sources of citations are important. Harry Truman was from Missouri—"the Show-Me" state. So, I will "show" you the source from which I formulated the question in case you want to read further. Actually, the correct answer(s) have multiple citations in my master draft of the manuscript. However, to limit the length of the book, I chose one "gold standard" citation for each question.

Remember that historians and biographers write and publish in a particular time frame. If you compared some writing on Truman soon after the detonation of the atom bombs in August 1945, you might find quite a dissonance with more recent historical interpretations, such as Richard B. Frank's *Downfall: The End of the Imperial Japanese Empire*; Frank had access to previously ignored and recently declassified sources that earlier authors had not had.

Historians, biographers, and history buffs, whether professional or amateur, interpret facts and events differently, particularly so in this era of "fake" facts, spin, and the notion that "I have a website so that makes me an expert!" As more researchers share their work in new books, articles, and lectures, some of us have to go back to the original materials for another look and interact with fresh sources of enlightenment.

Richard Lawrence Miller began his research believing Harry Truman was a "down-home sort of character with a refreshing honesty that seems absent from politics today." However, by the time Miller published *Truman: The Rise to Power* in 1986, he confessed, "I now must view him as a professional big-city machine politician involved in shady personal and political dealings" (1986, Preface). Moreover, Miller despaired of the self-appointed myth keepers who are uneasy with a rigorous exploration of Truman's involvement with the Pendergast machine in Kansas City. I disagree with Miller's interpretation of that period of Truman's life.

More recently, Stephen F. Knott closely examined the 1948 "come from behind" election. In *The Lost Soul of the American Presidency: The Decline into Demagoguery and the Prospects for Renewal*, (2019), Knott alleges that Truman "was willing to sow dissension, stir up fear, and slander his opponents," concluding, Truman "was a remarkably small and petty demagogue" (pp. 148–149). Thus, what he dismisses as "the campaign for beatification" ignited by widespread reading of David McCullough's bestseller *Truman* in 1992, "needs a healthy corrective" (p. 148). Having read other books on the election of 1948, I disagree with Knott.

Admittedly, over the quarter century plus since the publications of Miller and McCullough's views, archivists at the Harry S. Truman Presidential Library have uncovered and released materials to scholars that shed fresh light on dimensions of the 33rd president's life. This reality was demonstrated in 2016, when I sat through a spirited exchange between Sam Rushay, supervisory archivist at the Harry S. Truman Presidential Library, and an attendee of a lecture entitled "Brother Truman" which explored Truman's commitment to Masonry. At the conclusion of the lecture, during the question-and-answer segment, a visitor in the audience asked what resembled a question ("questions" in such venues are often commentary) about Truman's "poverty" upon leaving the White House. The questioner, not liking Rushay's answer, retorted, "Well, it's 'all over the internet' that Truman was broke when he came home to Independence." The archivist diplomatically cautioned that one cannot accept as fact everything "on the internet." The questioner, seemingly determined to correct the archivist, bristled, "But McCullough says..." [i.e., in *Truman*]. Rushay explained that although McCullough published *Truman* in 1992, he had conducted the research in the late 1980s. Simply, a lot of archival material has been released to researchers and published—and debated—in the decades since Truman sold farmland he owned as a way of lessening his financial stress; Truman did not receive a presidential pension until 1958. Obviously, David McCullough had not read these documents before writing his Pulitzer Prize-winning biography. This exchange became a valuable learning experience for me on the need to balance tested research with newer findings. Unfortunately, the questioner went away convinced that he was right. After adjourning, I congratulated Rushay on his diplomacy. Truman myths have tenacity and staying power and are passed down through generations, "My granddaddy told me that Truman did/ said...."

In the sources list for this book, readers will find few citations from internet websites. Certainly, citing them and relying on them might have made it easier for readers to back up their answers or to challenge my answers. Scholarly writing relies on an orderly process. An author may have graduate assistants or interns read drafts and do fact-checking. When the manuscript passes from the writer to a publisher, an editor and other members of the publishing team examine the manuscript carefully; indeed, a publisher may ask experts or content specialists to do a blind review of the text. A publisher may hire a fact-checker to verify the accuracy of the author's words, dates, spellings, and citations.

Fortunately, I have been blessed with a talented line editor, Mary Kay Speaks, who reads not just what is on the page but also what is *not* there. On more than one citation, she has emailed me: "I checked the source and your interpretation is not what I took away from reading it." That said, any mistakes in this book are mine.

Acknowledgments

Almost Everything Worth Knowing About Harry S Truman is a slight detour from another Truman book I am writing. While "Too many cooks spoil the broth" may be accurate about cooking, the writing and publishing of a book takes a cohort of people, often long-suffering souls who seemingly never tire of details about "the book," or the latest nugget of research.

First, I owe a great debt of gratitude to Mary Kay Speaks, whose skills as an editor are top drawer. If only she had been around to help Harry Truman with his memoirs. Special thanks to graphic artist Jack Martin whose superb layout skills made the manuscript more than just words on a page.

I am grateful for friends like Niel Johnson, Lee Ward, Arvil Pennington, Gerry Cox, Tim Cox, Dennis Apple, and John Larsen who read portions of early drafts. Gregory De-Bourgh offered incredible hours of proofreading, content analysis, and computer assistance.

I owe a tremendous debt to the presidential libraries where I have spent many hours reading, thinking. High marks go to the Harry S. Truman Presidential Library in Independence, Missouri. Not only does the HSTPL offer an amazing museum and expansive collections of Truman papers and materials, but gifted archivists led by Kurt Graham. I also wish to thank the Ronald Reagan Presidential Library in Simi Valley, California, the Dwight D. Eisenhower Presidential Library in Abilene, Kansas, the Richard Nixon Library in Yorba Linda, California, and the Franklin D. Roosevelt Presidential Library in Hyde Park, New York.

A great appreciation goes to the Truman Library Institute in Kansas City, led by my friend Alex Burden, executive director, and Clyde F. Wendel, board chair. The institute invites a rich cadre of speakers to lecture on various aspects of the life and political career of our 33rd president. One of the greatest "breathers" a writer can enjoy is the remarkable "Wild About Harry" fundraising dinner held every spring.

A special thanks to David McCullough, who jump-started my appreciation for Harry Truman with his monumental biography, *Truman*, and for his encouragement of this project with a simple phrase: "Keep at it. *Keep at it!*" His words have had the zing of a spirited cheerleader and nudged me in bringing order and creativity to the more than 500 questions—double-checking and triple-checking answers.

But this book would not have been possible without the incredible *Harry S. Truman Encyclopedia*, edited by Richard S. Kirkendall, professor emeritus of history, University of Washington. My copy has a broken spine, dog-eared pages, different colored underlines, but it has been a faithful friendly resource.

And a thank you to individuals who have shared "Harry Truman" stories, some of which are true.

This nation must never forget the tenacity, courage, patriotism, and fairness of Harry S Truman, the 33rd president of the United States.

Introduction

So how much do you know about Harry Truman, the 33rd president of the United States, who served from 1945–1953? Quite the man, quite the president.

No one after the bankruptcy of his clothing store in Kansas City in 1922 would have even imagined Harry Truman in the White House.

No one in November 1924, after his defeat for reelection as a judge of Jackson County, Missouri, would have imagined Harry Truman in the White House.

No one that hot summer of 1940, as Harry campaigned for reelection to the U.S. Senate, with no endorsement by FDR and no campaign funds—on occasion sleeping in his car because he didn't have money for a hotel room—would have imagined that Harry, within five years, would be in the White House.

And on one fateful April night, no one believed that the senator *Time* had described as "the mousy little man from Missouri" would be able to begin to fill the shoes of Franklin D. Roosevelt, let alone that he would be elected in his own right in 1948.

No one, during his eight years as president, would have predicted that, in time, historians would recognize Harry Truman as one of the country's "near-great" presidents.

The questions and facts making up this book demonstrate Truman's complexity, humanity, vision, and service to the country while providing readers a deeper understanding of "the man from Independence." Hopefully, this format provides an engaging and fun way to learn about the historical aspects of Truman's life. And, perhaps, readers will appreciate what a difference one man made.

Note: Throughout the manuscript the president's name will be Harry S Truman or HST.

Childhood

*Every morning at 5:00 a.m. HST
started his day doing what?*

1. Where was Harry S Truman (HST) born?
   A. Independence, Missouri
   B. Kansas City, Missouri
   C. Grandview, Missouri
   D. Lamar, Missouri

2. How many siblings did HST have?
   A. None
   B. Two
   C. Five
   D. Nine

3. What was HST's father's occupation?
   A. Farmer
   B. Mule and horse trader
   C. Carpenter
   D. Railroader

4. Every morning at 5:00 a.m. HST started his day doing what?
   A. Helping his mother prepare breakfast
   B. Milking cows
   C. Practicing piano for two hours
   D. Reading *The Independence Examiner*

5. Who reported that young HST had been "something of a sissy" as a boy?
   A. Margaret Truman
   B. Harry Truman
   C. David McCullough
   D. Bess Truman

6. Why did the Truman family move to Independence when HST was seven years old?
   A. Their farm was foreclosed
   B. For Harry to take advantage of better schools
   C. To attend First Presbyterian Church
   D. To live close to other Truman family members

7. When did HST's mother realize something was wrong with his eyesight?
    A. At a 4th of July celebration, he looked the opposite direction from the fireworks.
    B. Harry's continued difficulty sight-reading piano music
    C. Harry's difficulty reading schoolbooks
    D. Harry's teachers reported he could not see the chalkboards in the classroom.

8. HST's before-school job at Clinton's Drug Store on Independence Square included dusting, cleaning, and what?
    A. Slipping whiskey shots to pious businessmen
    B. Cleaning the bathroom
    C. Washing glassware
    D. Clipping articles out of newspapers he thought the druggist would find interesting

9. Charlie Ross, HST's best friend in Independence High School and a future winner of a Pulitzer Prize, filled what position in Truman's administration?
    A. Secretary of the Army
    B. Federal magistrate judge in Kansas City
    C. Press secretary
    D. Administrative aide for the budget

10. How did HST characterize his childhood?
    A. I "had the happiest childhood imaginable."
    B. "I had a childhood just like other boys had in that era."
    C. "There's not one thing I would change about my childhood."
    D. "Childhood in Independence, Missouri. Doesn't get any better than that."

15

11. What thwarted HST's dream of attending West Point?
    A. His mother's opposition as a pacifist
    B. The poor academic standards of Independence High School
    C. There were no vacancies in appointments from Missouri
    D. His poor eyesight

12. Martha Truman, at considerable expense, gave 10-year-old HST the four-volume, *Great Men and Famous Women*. What was the gift's lasting impact on HST?
    A. "Reading history to me was far more than a romantic adventure. It was solid instruction and wise teaching which I somehow felt that I wanted and needed."
    B. "That reading taught me that history makes 'great men.'"
    C. "There is no alternative to acting courageously."
    D. "Great leaders motivate great followers."

13. In 1957, Dean Acheson, in consultation with the past president of law librarians and Helen Lally of the U.S. Supreme Court Library, determined what about the *S* in HST's name?
    A. *S* is itself Truman's middle name.
    B. *S* stands for two men because Harry's parents could not choose.
    C. Harry had signed forms during World War I, Harry *Shippe* Truman.
    D. The *S* should not be punctuated with a period.

Childhood—*Answers*

1. D. Lamar, Missouri (Riley, 1989, p. 361)
2. B. Two (Riley, 1989, p. 362)
3. B. Mule and horse trader (Heller, 1989, p. 359)
4. C. Practicing piano for two hours (Walsh, 2005, p. 111)
5. B. Harry Truman (McCullough, 1992, p. 45)
6. B. For Harry to take advantage of better schools (Pemberton, 1989, p. xx)
7. A. At a 4th of July celebration, he looked the opposite direction from the fireworks. (McCullough, 1992, p. 41)
8. A. Slipping whiskey shots to pious businessmen (Truman, 1955, p. 122)
9. C. Press secretary (McCullough, 1992, p. 363)
10. A. I "had the happiest childhood imaginable." (McCullough, 1992, p. 39)
11. D. His poor eyesight (McCullough, 1992, p. 67)
12. A. "Reading history to me..." (Sullivan in Israel, 2004, pp. 351, 359)
13. A. *S* is itself Truman's middle name (Robbins, 1979, p. 46)

Young Adult

*As a young man, what gave HST
an opportunity to manage men
and an exposure to cursing?*

1. What item did HST never wear as a farmer?
   A. Long underwear
   B. Underwear made from flour sacks
   C. Overalls
   D. Clothes with zippers

2. Between high school graduation in 1901 and 1906 what did HST do?
   A. Worked on Grandview farms owned by relatives
   B. Worked at two banks in Kansas City
   C. Attended classes at University of Missouri
   D. Worked for several railroads

3. Which of the following properties was not owned, or partially owned, by HST?
   A. A house on Karnes Blvd. in Kansas City
   B. An apartment house at 39th and Bell
   C. A farm in Johnson County, Kansas
   D. A farm on Wornall Road in Kansas City

4. What organization did HST join in 1905?
   A. Benton Blvd. Baptist Church
   B. The National Guard
   C. Mike Pendergast's Tenth Ward Democratic Club
   D. The Jackson County Farm Bureau

5. When did HST return to work on the family farm?
   A. 1906
   B. 1910
   C. 1911
   D. 1916

6. What event in November 1914 impacted HST's life significantly?
   A. His grandmother Young died and willed him 125 acres
   B. His father, John Anderson Truman, died
   C. Bess Wallace began "courting" a wealthy Independence physician
   D. War broke out in Europe

7. How did the years on the farm impact HST?
   A. Gave him confidence to run a large farm
   B. Convinced him to take financial risks with his future
   C. Made him more gregarious and self-confident
   D. Convinced him that bankers had too much influence over farmers

8. As the economy boomed before the United States entered World War I, HST lost money in what business ventures?
   A. Land purchases along Sugar Creek in Independence
   B. Oil and mining businesses
   C. Development of property south of downtown Kansas City
   D. A general store in Grandview

9. What from HST's farm experience made him of interest to the military?
   A. His physical condition
   B. His experience with horses and mules
   C. His ability to manage money
   D. His leadership skills

10. As a young farmer, HST invested a great deal of his spare time doing what?
    A. Attending Masonic events
    B. Trading horses and mules
    C. Participating in agricultural contests
    D. Being active in the local Baptist church

11. On the farm, HST often prepared breakfast for farmhands. What was one lasting compliment of his cooking?
    A. "Harry cooked a breakfast that stuck to your ribs."
    B. "He fed you until you would just about burst."
    C. Harry could "stir up as good a batch of biscuits as any woman."

D. "Harry could have worked in *any* restaurant kitchen in Kansas City."

12. As a 20-year-old, HST rushed to see what celebrity in downtown Kansas City?
    A. Thomas Alva Edison
    B. Theodore Roosevelt
    C. William Jennings Bryan
    D. Wild Bill Hickok

13. As a young man, what gave HST an opportunity to manage men and an exposure to cursing?
    A. Working for a verbally abusive bank vice president
    B. Training with the National Guard
    C. Working as a timekeeper for a railroad work gang
    D. Ushering at Kansas City vaudeville performances

14. Soon after his father's death, HST was appointed to what position?
    A. Road overseer
    B. Secretary to presiding county judge
    C. Jackson County Agricultural Commission
    D. Grand Master, Grandview Masonic Lodge

15. After being appointed postmaster in Grandview, what did HST do?
    A. Built a new post office
    B. Delivered the mail by car
    C. Let a widow, who was raising young siblings, run the office and take the salary
    D. Returned his salary to the federal government

Young Adult—*Answers*

1. C. Overalls (Burnes, 2003, p. 23)

2. B. Worked at two banks in Kansas City (McCullough, 1992, p. 73)

3. D. A farm on Wornall Road in Kansas City (Hamby, 1995, pp. 93–94)

4. A. Benton Blvd. Baptist Church (Hamby, 1995, p. 21)

5. A. 1906 (Ferrell, 1983, p. 5)

6. B. His father, John Anderson Truman, died (Heller, 1989, p. 359)

7. A. Gave him confidence to run a large farm (Pemberton, 1989, p. 126)

   B. Convinced him to take financial risks with his future (Pemberton, 1989, p. 126)

   C. Made him more gregarious and self-confident (Pemberton, 1989, p. 126)

8. B. Oil and mining businesses (Johnson, 1989, p. 129)

9. B. His experience with horses and mules (Pemberton, 1989, p. 12)

10. A. Attending Masonic events (Roberts, 2012, pp. 14–15)

11. C. Harry could "stir up as good a batch of biscuits as any woman." (McCullough, 1992, p. 77)

12. B. Theodore Roosevelt (Beschloss, 2007, p. 213)

13. C. Working as a timekeeper for a railroad work gang (Melton, 1980, p. 11)

14. A. Road overseer (Robbins, 1979, p. 49)

15. C. Let a widow, who was raising young siblings, run the office and take the salary (Robbins, 1979, p. 50)

Soldier

What did HST do after returning home from World War I?

1. HST, 33, enlisted in the army during World War I. He could have been exempted because of what?
   A. Poor eyesight
   B. Occupation as a farmer
   C. Age
   D. Mother's health

2. During World War I HST visited Folies-Bergère in Paris. How did he later describe the show?
   A. Demeaning to women
   B. Disgusting
   C. Invigorating after the horrors of the battlefield
   D. Cheap and tawdry

3. How did HST dodge an incoming German shell that might have proved fatal?
   A. Moved his tent just before the shell landed
   B. Traded command posts with another captain
   C. Raided the mess hall for a midnight snack
   D. Played a poker game with fellow officers

4. HST's Battery D was made up of rowdy, boisterous, undisciplined what?
   A. Farm boys
   B. Irish-Catholics
   C. Polish-American Lutherans
   D. Individuals released from prison to serve in the army

5. Given his poor eyesight, how many pairs of eyeglasses did HST take to Europe?
   A. One
   B. Three
   C. Five
   D. Ten

6. How did HST's friendship with Eddie Jacobson begin?
   A. When they ran an army canteen
   B. When they both enlisted at the same time

C. When their fathers traded a horse
D. When Harry worked at a Kansas City bank and Jacobson was a client

7. HST faced down the Battery D noncommissioned officers, snapping, "I didn't come over here to get along with you!" and what else?
A. "Any one of you bastards want to take me on, man- to-man, come right ahead!"
B. "Get those sons of bitches under control or I will!"
C. "You've got to get along with me."
D. "I came over here to help win a war *not* to babysit grown men!"

8. How many of HST's men in Battery D died in France?
A. None
B. Two wounded; one died but from other causes
C. Five
D. Eight

9. What did HST do after returning home from World War I?
A. Worked as a bailiff at the Jackson County Court-house
B. Joined the American Legion
C. Sold his share of the Grandview farm for $15,000
D. Served as a clerk for the tax assessor

10. HST, as a veteran, was driven to achieve success to secure Bess's hand in marriage and what else?
A. To gain a reputation as a mover-and-shaker in Jackson County
B. To build contacts and friendships for a future political career
C. To win the "approval" of Bess's mother, Madge Wallace
D. To erase the reputation of his father as a financial "loser."

11. What did HST later say was based on his "war service and the friends he made during the war"?
    A. "My patriotism"
    B. "My sensitivity to veterans' needs and health care"
    C. "My political philosophy"
    D. "My whole political career"

12. Why did HST not return to farming after the war?
    A. He believed that farm prices would drop dramatically as government agricultural support shrank.
    B. He realized he could not achieve his political ambitions living in Grandview.
    C. He realized Bess did not want to be a farmer's wife.
    D. He considered his years as a farmer "a damn waste."

13. At one point in France, HST and Father L. Curtis Tiernan, a chaplain assigned to his unit, walked ahead of their soldiers and talked, among other things, "about the history of the world." What did HST tell the padre?
    A. "My deepest fears and deepest secrets"
    B. "If it wasn't for the Pope, I could be a Catholic"
    C. "If all priests were like [you], there wouldn't be any Protestants"
    D. "Padre, you could have made a good Baptist"

14. Toward the end of the war, when the Prince of Wales and General Pershing "reviewed" Truman's troops, what did one of HST's men say aloud?
    A. "Captain, ask them when we can go home?"
    B. "Captain, ask that little son of a bitch when he's going to free Ireland."
    C. "Captain, tell Pershing, if he ever comes to Kansas City we'll show him 'a good time.'"
    D. "Captain, ask the general if he knows how long we have been standing in this damn rain!"

Soldier—*Answers*

1. A. Poor eyesight (Dallek, 2008, p. 3)
   B. Occupation as a farmer (Dallek, 2008, p. 3)
   C. Age (Dallek, 2008, p. 3)
2. B. Disgusting (Ferrell, 1980/2002, p. 51)
3. A. Moved his tent just before the shell landed (Dallek, 2008, p. 49)
4. B. Irish-Catholics (Dunar, 1989, p. 24)
5. C. Five (Truman, 1955, p. 129)
6. D. When Harry worked at a Kansas City bank and Jacobson was a client (Bickerton, 1989, p. 186)
7. C. "You've got to get along with me." (McCullough, 1992, p. 117)
8. B. Two wounded; one died but from other causes (Hamby, 1995, p. 76)
9. C. Sold his share of the Grandview farm for $15,000 (Johnson, 1989, p. 129)
10. C. To win the "approval" of Bess's mother, Madge Wallace (Caroli, 1989, p. 358)
11. A. "My patriotism" (Dunar, 1989, p. 236)
    B. "My sensitivity to veterans' needs and health care" (Dunar, 1989, p. 236)
    C. "My political philosophy" (Dunar, 1989, p. 236)
    D. "My whole political career" (Dunar, 1989, p. 236)
12. C. He realized Bess did not want to be a farmer's wife. (Robbins, 1979, pp. 57–58)
13. C. "If all priests were like [you], there wouldn't be any Protestants." (McCullough, 1992, p. 127)
14. B. "Captain, ask that little son of a bitch when he's going to free Ireland." (Robbins, 1979, p. 33)

Family

*On one occasion HST put down
the newspaper and read
what book to his grandsons, ages
four and two?*

1. When Martha Truman visited the White House on Mother's Day 1945, how did she react to the attention and publicity?
   A. "I wouldn't have come if I'd known all these people were going to be here."
   B. "Where else would a president's mother want to be?"
   C. "You'd think I was the mother of Jesus!"
   D. "You must remember that I was Harry's mama long before he became president."

2. What [did] Martha Truman instill in her son Harry?
   A. The love of reading
   B. "Always do the right thing"
   C. The love of music, particularly the piano
   D. That some people were "too religious" to have as neighbors

3. What kept the ties strong between HST and his mother?
   A. His letters and phone calls
   B. His financial support
   C. Her ability to keep secrets and confidences
   D. Her belief that God had destined Harry to be successful

4. When Dr. Wallace Graham, the presidential physician, tried to tell HST that his mother had died, how did HST respond?
   A. "That cannot be right. She was getting better."
   B. He told the doctor that he knew she was dead because she just came to tell him goodbye.
   C. "Now I only have to make Bess and Margaret happy."
   D. "Well, there goes the vote I could always count on."

5. What belief did HST learn from his mother?
   A. "Never let the bank 'run' your business."
   B. "Late marriage has some benefits."
   C. "If a woman gets married, she should stay home
      and take care of the babies and the house."
   D. "It doesn't matter how beautiful a woman is if she
      can't cook!"

6. Martha Truman often told her son as he was leav-
   ing the farm, "Now Harry, you be good." What
   comment did she often add?
   A. "My boy wouldn't know how to be bad."
   B. "Being too good is apt to be uninteresting."
   C. "Young people have their own notions of 'being
      good.'"
   D. "Be the kind of man that Bess will admire."

7. On many Sundays HST, Bess, and Margaret went to
   Mama Truman's for what?
   A. Her midday fried chicken dinners
   B. A family picnic
   C. To attend church with Mama Truman
   D. To pick vegetables and pick up eggs

8. Who did HST often have to "arrange" jobs for?
   A. Fellow Masons
   B. Unemployed members of Battery D
   C. Neighbors in Independence
   D. His brother Vivian and two brothers-in-law

9. How old was HST when he became a grandfather?
   A. 64
   B. 69
   C. 73
   D. 76

10. How many grandchildren did HST and Bess have?
    A. One: Clifton

B. Three: Clifton, Martha, Harrison
C. Four: Clifton, Will, Harrison, Thomas
D. Five: Clifton, William, Margaret, Harris, Thomas

11. On one occasion HST put down the newspaper and read what book to his grandsons, ages four and two?
A. *Bible Study for Boys and Girls*
B. *The Adventures of Tom Sawyer*
C. *The Iliad*
D. Thucydides' *History of the Peloponnesian War*

12. Where was HST when he learned his mother had died?
A. In a cabinet meeting
B. Addressing a group of union leaders
C. Flying over Ohio
D. Shaving in the White House

13. When Martha Truman died in 1947, the press speculated on what?
A. The true nature of the relationship between Martha and Bess
B. How much money she left the president
C. Her lasting influence on HST
D. With Martha dead, would he run in 1948

Family—*Answers*

1. A. "I wouldn't have come if I'd known all these people were going to be here." (Riley, 1989, p. 361)

2. A. The love of reading (Riley, 1989, p. 361)

   B. "Always do the right thing" (Riley, 1989, p. 361)

   C. The love of music, particularly the piano (Riley, 1989, p. 361)

   D. That some people were "too religious" to have as neighbors (Riley, 1989, p. 361)

3. A. His letters and phone calls (Riley, 1989, p. 361)

4. B. He told the doctor that he knew she was dead because she just came to tell him goodbye. (McCullough, 1992, p. 571)

5. C. "If a woman gets married, she should stay home and take care of the babies and the house." (Riley, 1989, p. 361)

6. B. "Being too good is apt to be uninteresting." (Truman, 1973, p. 540)

7. A. Her midday fried chicken dinners (Truman, 1996, p. 109)

8. D. His brother Vivian and two brothers-in-law (McCullough, 1992, p. 176)

9. C. 73 (McCullough, 1992, p. 960)

10. C. Four: Clifton, Will, Harrison, Thomas (Daniel, 1995, pp. 220–228)

11. D. Thucydides' *History of the Peloponnesian War* (Truman, 1973, p. 573)

12. C. Flying over Ohio (McCullough, 1992, p. 571)

13. C. Her lasting influence on HST (Riley, 1989, p. 361)

Harry, Bess, and Margaret

Why did HST stop playing the piano in public?

1. Where did Harry first see Bess Wallace?
   A. Sunday School class at First Presbyterian Church, Independence
   B. Pie supper at the Jackson County Fair
   C. A spelling bee at the Independence City Hall
   D. When she was visiting his cousin

2. Why did HST not marry Bess before going off to World War I?
   A. His lack of money
   B. His financial distress
   C. His fear that he might come home maimed or crippled
   D. Her mother's vigorous objections

3. On June 28, 1919, where were HST and Bess Wallace married?
   A. First Baptist Church, Independence
   B. Parlor in Bess's home
   C. Trinity Episcopal Church, Independence
   D. Jackson County Courthouse, Independence

4. How old was HST when he married Bess Wallace?
   A. 31
   B. 32
   C. 35
   D. 36

5. What did Madge Wallace, HST's mother-in-law, always call him?
   A. "Mr. Truman"
   B. "The Judge"
   C. "That dirt-poor farmer"
   D. "Bess's husband"

6. Why did HST stop playing the piano in public?
   A. The music critic of *The New York Times* quipped "Harry Truman was president not the 'first pianist'!"

B. Bess pitched a fit after he was photographed playing at the National Press Club as Lauren Bacall perched on the piano lid.
C. He was getting too many invitations to play for symphonies for fundraisers.
D. He never had time to practice and his playing showed.

7. When an individual critiqued Bess's increasingly "matronly" figure, how did HST react?
   A. "She looks just the way a woman of her age ought to look."
   B. "Say one more word and you are going to have a black eye."
   C. "That, sir, is none of your business."
   D. "She's the first lady, not some Hollywood floozy!"

8. What did HST call his wife?
   A. "God's greatest gift to me"
   B. "The Boss"
   C. "Mrs. Truman"
   D. "The Warden"

9. How did HST describe his mother-in-law?
   A. "A grand lady"
   B. "Bess's mother and Margaret's grandmother"
   C. "A good candidate for mother-of-the-year"
   D. "A gift that I have learned to appreciate"

10. What did Bess identify as the duties of a first lady?
    A. "To make her husband happy when everyone else is making him mad."
    B. "To sit beside her husband and be silent and be sure her hat is on straight."
    C. "To make sure my husband looks good and make everyone think how brilliant he was to marry me."
    D. "To make certain he doesn't get too big for his britches."

11. What did Bess Truman say about public expecta-
tions of her as first lady?
    A. "I am NO Eleanor Roosevelt!"
    B. "I'm not going down into any coal mines."
    C. "Harry wears the pants in *this* family! Always has,
       always will."
    D. "Don't expect me to go gallivanting around the
       country like other first ladies."

12. One morning, after returning the previous evening
to the White House from a trip to Independence,
what did a chagrinned Bess report to Chief Usher
J. B. West?
    A. That Mrs. Nesbitt seemed to answer incessantly,
       "Mrs. Roosevelt never did it *that* way."
    B. That daughter Margaret's college friends would be,
       at times, "messy, loud, and demanding."
    C. All meals in the White House must conform to
       wartime rationing regulations
    D. The president's antique bed had collapsed

13. What was one negative aspect of what Bess called
"First Ladying"?
    A. Presiding over large events "packed with hundreds
       of overheated committee women"
    B. VIPS who demanded personal White House tours
    C. Individuals wanting her to donate personal items
       for charity fundraisers
    D. Countless requests to send "words of welcome" to
       women's conventions and conferences

14. According to Chief Usher J. B. West, if Mrs. Truman was in residence, what often happened at 9:00
p.m.?
    A. "The president picked up his briefcase, took Mrs.
       Truman by the arm, went into his study, and
       closed the door."

B. Mrs. Truman "called it a night."

C. The president often asked what dessert might be available.

D. The president summoned the chief usher and said, "That will be all. Good night."

15. If Bess Truman was "the boss," who was the boss's boss?

A. Harry Truman

B. Margaret Truman

C. Madge Wallace

D. No one "bossed" the boss

16. To what was Margaret Truman referring when she mentioned "The White House Blues"?

A. Bess Truman had to confront the new reality that she had become a spectator rather than a partner in Harry's presidency.

B. Bess could do few things spontaneously or without Secret Service approval

C. Bess and Margaret wondered, on any given day, what Georgetown insiders were saying about them.

D. The lack of ease their friends felt when visiting them in the White House

17. After HST was nominated as a candidate for vice president, when asked, "What have you done while Harry was a politician?" how did Bess answer?

A. "Me? I've been watching out for lowlifes that wanted something from him."

B. "I've been keeping him focused on his voters."

C. "I've been in politics for the last 25 years."

D. "I've been taking care of my mother, my daughter, my husband, and our home in Independence."

18. Bess, even in retirement, kept up with politics. In 1973, a historian visiting at the Truman Library informed her that President Nixon's mining Haiphong

Harbor was probably "a good decision." Nodding toward HST, who supported Nixon's policy, how did Bess respond?

A. "Harry, I think you and Nixon are crazy as hell!"
B. "If he were president, we would have done it six years ago."
C. "Harry would have done a hell of lot more than 'mine' some harbor."
D. "Could I ask you to put that in writing?"

19. What was Bess's twist on HST's maxim, "If you can't stand the heat, get out of the kitchen"?
A. "Move to Alaska or Minnesota."
B. "Kitchen? Harry Truman hasn't been in a kitchen more than to make toast."
C. "If it's too hot for me, I'll get back to the kitchen."
D. "If you can't stand the heat, then crank up the air conditioning!"

20. On what occasion did aide Harry Vaughn report to HST: "Mrs. Truman looked like you do when you draw four aces"?
A. Presidential inaugural parade, 1949
B. After the Jefferson-Jackson Dinner when HST announced he would not be a candidate for president in 1952
C. At daughter Margaret's wedding
D. After her first grandson's birth

21. What three lessons did Margaret Truman learn living in the White House as first daughter?
A. She was "public property."
B. She could not go anywhere without a Secret Service agent.
C. Say "as little as possible" if reporters were nearby
D. Any chance for romance was remote.

22. After General Eisenhower had been sworn in as

president, as the Trumans were being driven to a farewell luncheon, Margaret surprised her father by saying what?

A. "That was one hell of a way to spend eight years!"
B. "Daddy, you just got a 'Get out of jail free card.'"
C. "Hello, Mr. Truman!"
D. "Whatever you are called—you will always be 'Daddy' to me."

23. As Bess and HST entered their home for the first time as former president and first lady, what did Bess say to her husband?"

A. "Now, Harry, I don't have to share you with anybody."
B. "Are you sure, we're home for good?"
C. "If this is what you get for all those years of hard work I guess it was worth it."
D. "Why don't we sleep in tomorrow? Haven't we earned that?"

24. Responding to a written question submitted about what she would wear to a certain event, the first lady scribbled what answer?

A. She always waited until the last minute to choose clothes for major events.
B. What she wore was "nobody's d[amned] business."
C. She might buy something special to wear for this event.
D. She could not imagine that anyone was interested in what she would wear.

25. What did HST give Margaret for her eighth birthday that caused her to cry?

A. A pony
B. A train set
C. A grand piano
D. Her own set of *Great Men and Famous Women*

26. HST banned what influential woman from White House functions because of her unflattering comments about Bess?

A. Congresswoman Clare Boothe Luce
B. Alice Roosevelt Longworth
C. Francis Perkins
D. Mary Bethune

27. When reporters pressed for "more" background information from the new first lady, how did Bess respond?

A. "Mrs. Harry Truman should be ample."
B. "You don't need to know me. I'm only the president's wife and the mother of his daughter."
C. "Here you go: Daughter, mother, wife, Democrat, bridge player, reader of mysteries—oh, yeah, and first lady."
D. "The girl that is crazy about Harry Truman."

28. What did HST say about Bess's involvement in his political career?

A. "Bess kept me focused on the main thing."
B. "I discussed all of them [major decisions] with her. Why not? Her judgment was always good."
C. "Bess always had a way of reminding me who I was, where I was from, and where, someday, I would be returning."
D. "Bess had a keen sense of what housewives wanted."

29. What nickname did the Secret Service assign the Trumans?

A. The Missourians
B. The Mule Team
C. The Jacksonians
D. The Three Musketeers

30. Bess's example of independence as first lady influenced what future resident of 1600 Pennsylvania Avenue?
    A. Mamie Eisenhower
    B. Lady Bird Johnson
    C. Betty Ford
    D. Rosalyn Carter

31. What did Margaret and Bess tell HST about the election of 1952?
    A. "Get used to the idea that the next president is going to be a Republican!"
    B. You are "the only Democrat who can win the presidency."
    C. "If you run for another term the two women in your life will be a widow and an orphan."
    D. "Eisenhower's 'coattails' will be a tidal wave."

32. How did the Truman family select musical artists to play for White House/Blair House events?
    A. Harry chose pianists
    B. Bess chose violinists
    C. Margaret chose vocalists
    D. Any artist had to be approved by two of the three Trumans

33. Why did Bess Truman defer to professional decorators when the White House was restored?
    A. "It would be unfair to the next First Lady to impose too many of my ideas upon the house."
    B. "I am very aware that my home is in Independence and is *not* the White House."
    C. "I only live, at the moment, in government housing."
    D. "If I would even make even a suggestion, 20 women in Georgetown will look down their noses at me."

34. Learning that Margaret was going to marry a news-man, after a period of silence, what did HST say?

A. "He's not one of those newsmen like that damn Drew Pearson is he?"

B. "Well, if you love him, that's good enough for me."

C. "Does your mama know about this? She's not too keen on reporters."

D. "He is a Democrat, right?"

Harry, Bess, and Margaret—*Answers*

1. A. Sunday School class at First Presbyterian Church, Independence (Truman, 1953, p. 128)
2. C. His fear that he might come home maimed or crippled (McCullough, 1992, p. 103)
3. C. Trinity Episcopal Church, Independence (Taylor, 2013, p. 41)
4. C. 35 (Taylor, 2013, p. 41)
5. A. "Mr. Truman" (Beschloss, May 8, 2014)
6. B. Bess pitched a fit after he was photographed playing at the National Press Club as Lauren Bacall perched on the piano lid. (Witcover, 2014, p. 333; McCullough, 1992, p. 337)
7. A. "She looks just the way a woman of her age ought to look." (Caroli, 1995, p. 209)
8. B. "The Boss" (Caroli, 1989, p. 354)
9. A. "A grand lady" (Beschloss, May 8, 2014)
10. B. "To sit beside her husband and be silent and be sure her hat is on straight." (Walsh, 2005, p. 108)
11. B. "I'm not going down into any coal mines." (Anthony, September 4, 2013)
12. D. The president's antique bed had collapsed (McCullough, 1992, p. 750)
13. A. Presiding over large events "packed with hundreds of overheated committee women" (Anthony, September 4, 2013)
14. A. "The president picked up his briefcase, took Mrs. Truman by the arm, went into his study, and closed the door." (Giangreco & Moore, 1999, p. 9)
15. B. Margaret Truman (Withers, 1996, p. 192)
16. A. Bess Truman had to confront the new reality that she had become a spectator rather than a partner in Harry's presidency. (Caroli, 1995, p. 89)

17. C. "I've been in politics for the last 25 years." (Truman, 2004, p. 148)

18. B. "If he were president, we would have done it six years ago." (Truman, 2004, p. 148)

19. C. "If it's too hot for me, I'll get back to the kitchen." (Truman, 2004, p. 188)

20. B. After the Jefferson-Jackson Dinner when HST announced he would not be a candidate for president in 1952 (Uebelhor, 2006, p. 586)

21. A. She was "public property." (Truman, 2004, p. 233)

    B. She could not go anywhere without a Secret Service agent. (Truman, 2004, p. 233)

    C. Say "as little as possible" if reporters were nearby (Truman, 2004, p. 233)

22. C. "Hello, Mr. Truman!" (Truman, 1973, p. 558)

23. C. "If this is what you get for all those years of hard work I guess it was worth it." (Truman, 1953, p. 24)

24. B. "What she wore was nobody's d[amned] business." (Anthony, September 4, 2013)

25. C. A grand piano (Robbins, 1979, p. 73)

26. A. Congresswoman Clare Boothe Luce (Robbins, 1979, p. 45)

27. B. "You don't need to know me. I'm only the president's wife and the mother of his daughter." (Brower, 2016, p. 11)

28. B. "I discussed all of them [major decisions] with her. Why not? Her judgment was always good." (Caroli, 1995, p. 204)

29. D. The Three Musketeers (Caroli, 1995, p. 203)

30. C. Betty Ford (Ellis, 2008, p. 262)

31. B. You are "the only Democrat who could win the presidency." (Beschloss, 2018, p. 446)

32. A. Harry chose pianists (Spann & Williams, 2008, p. 225)

    B. Bess chose violinists (Spann & Williams, 2008, p. 225)

C. Margaret chose vocalists (Spann & Williams, 2008, p. 225)

33. A. "It would be unfair to the next First Lady to impose too many of my ideas upon the house." (Seale, 2008, p. 1044)

34. B. "Well, if you love him, that's good enough for me." (Truman, 2003, p. 337)

County Judge

*How did Truman respond to a
Klan threat against him?*

1. The first book HST wrote, *Results of County Planning*, was on what topic?
   A. Strengthening public confidence in county government
   B. Ways to enhance landscape through progress
   C. Encouraging population growth
   D. Making county government more efficient

2. HST helped the Republican National Committee raise money for the convention which nominated who for president?
   A. Dwight Eisenhower
   B. Thomas Dewey
   C. Richard Nixon
   D. Herbert Hoover

3. Approximately how many miles of new concrete highways did HST build as Jackson County judge?
   A. 103 miles
   B. 224 miles
   C. 503 miles
   D. 671 miles

4. The Ku Klux Klan, in 1922, promised to support HST for county judge if he would promise that he would never hire...?
   A. Immigrants
   B. Catholics
   C. Jews
   D. Negroes

5. What did *not* contribute to HST's victory as eastern county judge of Jackson County?
   A. Veterans and kinfolk residing in nearly every precinct
   B. Voters sympathized with a man who admitted his financial history
   C. People liked Harry; Harry liked people
   D. Harry's spellbinding speeches on the stump

6. In 1926, HST ran for presiding judge of Jackson County instead of what office that paid more?
   A. County collector
   B. Sheriff
   C. County treasurer
   D. Road commissioner

7. Given the county's enormous debt, how did HST as presiding judge, anger local bankers?
   A. Threatened to default on county bonds
   B. Negotiated lower interest rates with St. Louis and Chicago banks
   C. Called attention to the lifestyles of the bankers
   D. Demanded they lighten up on declaring farms in default

8. Determined to build one of the finest county court-houses in North America, what did HST do?
   A. Hired a famous architect to advise him
   B. Drove 24,000 miles, at his own expense, to inspect new courthouses
   C. Personally supervised construction
   D. Declared he would "bring in the project on budget or resign"

9. HST wanted a statue of what American hero for the front of the new courthouse? Obsessed over historical accuracy, he traveled to what former president's home to make measurements?
   A. George Washington
   B. U. S. Grant
   C. Andrew Jackson
   D. Zachary Taylor

10. Although HST approved new roads cutting through 11 acres of his mother's farm, what did he do?
    A. Paid her the usual reimbursement of the county

B. Paid her the usual reimbursement plus $1

C. Promised to name the highway for her

D. Denied her any compensation

11. Periodically, where did Harry sleep to avoid being hounded for jobs?
    A. In his old bedroom on the Grandview farm
    B. In unregistered rooms in downtown hotels
    C. On a cot in the Jackson County home for orphan children
    D. In a VIP cell at the Jackson County Jail

12. On the eve of HST's 1930 reelection, what shook the presiding judge and Bess?
    A. The death of his friend Mike Pendergast
    B. A KKK rally that targeted him
    C. An attempted kidnapping of daughter, Margaret
    D. The collapse of the stock market

13. HST calculated that he could have "pocketed" how much money as presiding judge of Jackson County?
    A. $50,000
    B. $100,000
    C. $250,000
    D. $1,500,000

14. As judge, HST had more than 7,000 seedling pop-lars and elm trees planted along new roads he built. What eventually happened to those trees?
    A. They still grow beside HST-built roads
    B. Farmers mowed them down
    C. Many ended up fence posts on farms
    D. Years later many were used to make picnic tables for parks in Jackson County

15. How did Truman respond to a Klan threat against him?
    A. Bought a full-page advertisement in *The Independence Examiner* and rebutted their allegations
    B. Went to a Klan gathering, stood up, and vigorously denounced their bigotry
    C. Took off his jacket, rolled up his sleeves, and yelled, "Come on you yellow sons-of-bitches. Come up here and say it to my face and see what happens!"
    D. Asked Boss Pendergast to send thugs to provide "physical exercise" for the Klansmen at the rally

County Judge—*Answers*

1. B. Ways to enhance landscape through progress (Mc-Cullough, 1992, p. 177)
2. D. Herbert Hoover (McCullough, 1992, p. 175)
3. B. 224 miles (McCullough, 1992, pp. 176, 244; Taylor, 2013, p. 86)
4. B. Catholics (McCullough, 1992, p. 164)
   C. Jews (Robbins, 1979, p. 61)
5. A. Veterans and kinfolk residing in nearly every precinct (Robbins, 1979, p. 60)
6. A. County collector (McCullough, 1992, p. 173)
7. B. Negotiated lower interest rates with St. Louis and Chicago banks (Truman, 1955, p. 139)
8. B. Drove 24,000 miles, at his own expense, to inspect new courthouses (Robbins, 1979, p. 73; McCullough, 1992, p. 178)
9. C. Andrew Jackson (Hillman, 1984, p. 205)
10. D. Denied her any compensation (Hedley, 1979, p. 284; Robbins, 1979, p. 73)
11. A. In his old bedroom on the Grandview farm (Hamby, 1995, p. 167)
    B. In unregistered rooms in downtown hotels
12. C. An attempted kidnapping of daughter, Margaret (McCullough, 1992, p. 183)
13. D. $1,500,000 (McCullough, 1992, p. 187)
14. B. Farmers mowed them down (McCullough, 1992, p. 177)
15. B. Went to a Klan gathering, stood up, and vigorously denounced their bigotry (Robbins, 1979, p. 61)

U.S. Senator

Why did HST threaten to throw Joseph P. Kennedy out a hotel window?

1. Why did HST run for the Senate in 1934?
   A. Failed to gain Pendergast's endorsement to run for the House of Representatives
   B. Needed a job
   C. To gain statewide recognition to eventually run for governor
   D. To prevent foreclosure on his debt

2. Who offered HST this advice: "Work hard, keep your mouth shut, and answer your mail!"
   A. Martha Truman
   B. Vice President John Nance Garner
   C. Governor Guy Brasfield Park
   D. Tom Pendergast

3. Early in his Senate term, what was HST derisively called?
   A. "The Senator from Pendergast"
   B. "Big Tom's little errand boy"
   C. "The *dis*honorable gentleman from Missouri"
   D. "The failed haberdasher"

4. Having what person on his senate payroll could have become a controversial campaign issue?
   A. Margaret Truman
   B. Bess Truman
   C. Tom Pendergast, Jr.
   D. Jimmy Roosevelt

5. During HST's 1940 Senate reelection campaign, when he was unable to attract campaign donations, what did he do?
   A. Borrowed on his life insurance
   B. Occasionally slept in his car
   C. Held a radio fundraiser
   D. Accepted a large check from Bernard Baruch

6. Who did not endorse HST's 1940 Senate reelection campaign?
   A. FDR
   B. Joel B. Clark, the other U.S. Senator from Missouri
   C. Charles Keith, interim mayor of Kansas City
   D. Robert E. Hannagan, Democratic powerbroker in Missouri

7. HST believed three realities could tarnish a senator's reputation. Which element did he not include?
   A. Money
   B. Power
   C. Women
   D. Liquor

8. How did HST describe Lloyd Stark, the governor of Missouri, who had promised not to run against him for the Democratic nomination for Senate in 1940?
   A. "A lying, scheming, two-timing no good bastard"
   B. "A weasel and a hypocrite!"
   C. "A son of a bitch"
   D. "One despicable excuse of a public servant"

9. Why did HST threaten to throw Joseph P. Kennedy out a hotel window?
   A. Kennedy had insulted Bess's matronly figure
   B. Kennedy had sent a prostitute to Harry's hotel room
   C. Kennedy had offered Harry a large bribe
   D. Kennedy had called FDR "a crippled son of a bitch" in Truman's presence

10. Why did HST not socialize more in Washington as a senator?
    A. He was socially inept.
    B. He said there was "more work to do than 96 men could ever keep up with."
    C. Bess was nervous in social settings.
    D. Bess spent a lot of the year back in Independence.

11. Which of the following was *not* a contribution of the "Truman Committee" HST chaired from 1941–1944?
   A. Saved billions of tax dollars
   B. Key source of information about domestic elements of the war effort
   C. Increased public confidence in the conduct of the war
   D. Promoted profiles of celebrity soldiers

12. Senator Truman put tens of thousands of miles on his own car doing what?
   A. Investigating military and defense installations
   B. Campaigning for other Democrats
   C. Lining up support for a future presidential bid
   D. Speaking at Democratic events for honorariums to supplement his Senate salary

13. While serving in the Senate HST was named what?
   A. "The best-read senator."
   B. "One of the 10 best-dressed senators."
   C. "The senator most likely to end up in the White House."
   D. "The hardest-working member of the Senate."

14. What embarrassed HST in 1940 when he ran for reelection to the Senate?
   A. Three of his staff had been indicted for fraud.
   B. Boss Tom Pendergast boasted that he intended to vote twice for Harry.
   C. Four large personal checks bounced at the bank.
   D. His mother's farm was foreclosed.

15. The Truman Committee is estimated to have saved U.S. taxpayers how much money?
   A. $82 million
   B. $250 million
   C. $1 billion for every year of the war
   D. $15 billion

16. HST claimed that the Truman Committee not only saved billions of taxpayer dollars, but also saved what?
    A. The lives of thousands of fighting men
    B. The integrity of the Department of War
    C. The reputation of FDR
    D. Hundreds of war industries from being infiltrated by spies

17. How did HST summarize his decade in the U.S. Senate?
    A. "The best venue to understand the workings of the federal government."
    B. "A conscience-stretching decade, to say the least."
    C. "Happiest 10 years of my life"
    D. "A golden opportunity to serve with some of the finest statesmen in America."

18. What "prize" did FDR and Washington insiders dangle if HST would drop out of the 1940 Senate race?
    A. Governor of Samoa
    B. Secretary of War
    C. Secretary of Agriculture in the third term
    D. Appointment to the Interstate Commerce Commission

19. Where did HST say, "Jews, are being herded into the ghettos, the concentration camps, and the wastelands of Europe.... Today, not tomorrow, we must do all that is humanly possible to provide a haven and a place of safety for all those who can be grasped from the hands of the Nazi butchers."
    A. Mass rally in Chicago, April 14, 1943
    B. Truman Committee hearing, February 3, 1942
    C. In a speech on the Senate floor, August 16, 1943
    D. In a meeting with the secretary of state

20. How much did HST earn as a U.S. Senator when he began his first term in 1935?
    A. $5,000 per year
    B. $7,500 per year
    C. $10,000 per year
    D. $20,000 per year

21. What honor did HST receive in 1943?
    A. Honorary doctorate from Harvard
    B. *Time* named him "Man of the Year"
    C. American Mason of the Year Award
    D. A place sitting beside FDR at a White House state dinner

22. What were among Bess's duties in HST's Senate office?
    A. Sorted mail
    B. Counseled him on certain issues
    C. Proofread drafts of speeches
    D. Reached out to potential donors in Missouri

23. What resource did HST find valuable in chairing the Truman Committee?
    A. Poker-playing pals in the War and Navy departments
    B. *The Report of the Civil War Committee on the Conduct of the War*
    C. *The Art of War*, Chinese military treatise from the fifth century BC
    D. *The Personal Memoirs of Ulysses S. Grant*

24. How much money was HST initially given to investigate the $25 billion defense spending?
    A. $15,000
    B. $50,000
    C. $100,000
    D. Whatever he needed to fund the committee's work

25. When Claire Boothe Luce lambasted Bess as "Payroll Bess," how did Truman defend her work?

A. "Hell, every senator has family members on staff."
B. "If John Nance Garner can do it, why can't I?"
C. "Mrs. Luce wouldn't last a day in my office."
D. "She...does much of my clerical work. I need her there and that's the reason I've got her there."

26. As a senator, what assessment of FDR did HST and Bess share?

A. "You can take the man out of the Hudson Valley but you can't take the Hudson Valley aristocracy out of the man!"
B. "He is so damn afraid he won't have all the power and glory that he won't let his friends help as it should be done."
C. "God's right-hand man!"
D. "One complex son of a bitch!"

U.S. Senator—*Answers*

1. A. Failed to gain Pendergast's endorsement to run for the House of Representatives (Truman, 1955, p. 141)
2. D. Tom Pendergast (McCullough, 1992, p. 213)
3. A. "The Senator from Pendergast" (Baime, 2017, p. 76)
4. B. Bess Truman (Burnes, 2003, p. 126)
5. A. Borrowed on his life insurance (McCullough, 1992, p. 245)
    B. Occasionally slept in his car (McCullough, 1992, p. 245)
    D. Accepted a large check from Bernard Baruch (Neiberg, 2016, p. 8)
6. A. FDR (McCullough, 1992, p. 241)
7. D. Liquor (Robbins, 1980, p. 183)
8. C. "A son of a bitch" (McCullough, 1992, p. 230)
9. D. Kennedy had called FDR "a crippled son of a bitch" in Truman's presence (McCullough, 1992, p. 230)
10. B. He said there was "more work to do than 96 men could ever keep up with." (Truman, 1955, p. 146)
    D. Bess spent a lot of the year back in Independence. (Ferrell, 1983, p. 180)
11. A. Saved billions of tax dollars (Heath, 1989, p. 364)
    C. Increased public confidence in the conduct of the war (Heath, 1989, p. 364)
12. A. Investigating military and defense installations (Truman, 1955, p. 165)
13. B. "One of the 10 best-dressed senators." (Richardson, July 5, 2019)
14. D. His mother's farm was foreclosed. (Taylor, 2013, p. 71)
15. D. $15 billion (Heath, 1989, p. 364)
16. A. The lives of thousands of fighting men (Robbins, 1979, p. 87)

17. C. "Happiest 10 years of my life" (Koterba, September 2, 1960, p. 18)

18. D. Appointment to the Interstate Commerce Commission (Truman, 1973, p. 120; McCullough, 1992, p. 241)

19. A. Mass rally in Chicago, April 14, 1943 (Breitman & Lichtman, 2013, p. 222)

20. C. $10,000 (Robbins, 1979, p. 79)

21. B. *Time* named him "Man of the Year" (Kundhardt, 1999, p. 250; Hamby, 1995, p. 260)

22. A. Sorted mail (Robbins, 1979, p. 49)

   B. Counseled him on certain issues (Robbins, 1979, p. 49)

   C. Proofread drafts of speeches (Robbins, 1979, p. 49)

23. B. *The Report of the Civil War Committee on the Conduct of the War* (Robbins, 1979, p. 86)

24. A. $15,000 (Ferrell, 1983, p. 33)

25. D. "She ...does much of my clerical work. I need her there and that's the reason I've got her there." (Caroli, 1995, p. 207; *The New York Times*, July 27, 1944, p. 11)

26. B. "He's so damn afraid that he won't have all the power and glory that he won't let his friends help as it should be done." (Beschloss, 2018, p. 443)

Vice President

Although HST enjoyed presiding over the Senate, he had difficulty accepting what?

1. HST did not want to be FDR's running mate in 1944. His ambition was for what office?

   A. Governor of Missouri
   B. Reelection as senator from Missouri in 1946
   C. Secretary of Agriculture
   D. Director, Library of Congress

2. Which of the following was *not* a reason FDR selected HST as his running mate in 1944?

   A. FDR thought HST's popularity in the Senate would help in lining up ratification of a peace treaty.
   B. Truman was popular in all factions of Democratic Party.
   C. HST's support of New Deal pleased labor and Northern liberals.
   D. HST was a bitter enemy of Henry Wallace.

3. According to Margaret Truman, why did HST resist running with FDR who he knew was ill?

   A. HST did not want to go into the White House "through the back door."
   B. HST did not want to give up chairing the Truman Committee before its work was completed.
   C. HST resented that he had survived a tough reelection to the Senate without FDR's endorsement in 1940.
   D. Vice presidents just sit around "waiting for something bad to happen."

4. After HST became Roosevelt's running mate in 1944, how did *Time* magazine describe him?

   A. "A man of distinct limitations"
   B. "Vice President *Who?*"
   C. "The mousy little man from Missouri"
   D. "The broke failed haberdasher"

5. What did FDR forbid HST to do during the campaign?

   A. Travel by airplane

   B. Make any large personal purchases

   C. Criticize the Roosevelt sons

   D. Voice enthusiasm for civil rights in any way

6. Where did Truman take his oath as vice president?

   A. East steps of the U.S. Capitol

   B. The Capitol rotunda

   C. South portico of the White House

   D. In the well of the U.S. Senate

7. What advice did HST's mother offer him after he was sworn in as vice president in 1945?

   A. "Now, you behave yourself."

   B. "Finally, you are done with that crook Pendergast!"

   C. "Keep your eye on Roosevelt. He's known to change his mind."

   D. "Keep Bess and Margaret happy."

8. How long did HST serve as vice president?

   A. 47 days

   B. 82 days

   C. 96 days

   D. 367 days

9. Although HST enjoyed presiding over the Senate, he had difficulty accepting what?

   A. He was the first vice president to be assigned Secret Service protection.

   B. He could only vote in case of a tie.

   C. He had to listen to "windbags" and egoists.

   D. Tourists in the gallery gawked at him.

10. Why did Harry's attendance at Tom Pendergast's funeral in Kansas City in 1945 create such controversy?

   A. People had made cash wagers that he would *not* attend.
   B. Ushers were being slipped money to be seated close to HST.
   C. Pendergast associates put up money for a rowdy "bourbon" wake at the Muehlebach Hotel which Truman attended.
   D. Many thought that he demeaned the dignity of the office of vice president.

11. While vice president where did HST reside?

   A. In an apartment at 4701 Connecticut Avenue
   B. In a suite at the Willard Hotel
   C. Blair House
   D. The Naval Observatory

12. How did HST describe the office of vice president?

   A. The one office "in which it is the man who makes the office, not the office the man"
   B. An office of "anomalous insignificance and curious uncertainty"
   C. "Not worth a pitcher of warm spit"
   D. "A graveyard for the politically ambitious."

13. HST worried about what "ghost in the closet" being uncovered by reporters during the 1944 campaign?

   A. Suicide of Bess's father
   B. Details of his bankruptcy
   C. Undisclosed business deals with Pendergast
   D. That Kansas City tailors made his suits free of charge

14. How long did HST's acceptance speech of the Democratic vice presidential nomination last?

   A. 20 minutes

B. 10 minutes

C. 5 minutes

D. 1 minute

15. How did HST assess the duties of the vice president?

A. "It's a high profile, dead-end job."

B. "Serving as the president's errand boy to Congress."

C. "The VP simply presides over the Senate and sits around hoping for a funeral."

D. "It's like being hung by the neck until dead. Only you have to go back up the gallows the next morning."

Vice President—*Answers*

1. B. Reelection as a senator from Missouri in 1946 (McCullough, 1992, p. 308)
2. D. HST was a bitter enemy of Henry Wallace. (Kirkendall, 1989, p. 383)
3. A. HST did not want to go into the White House "through the back door." (Truman, 1973, p. 190)
4. C. "The mousy little man from Missouri" (McCullough, 1992, p. 320)
5. A. Travel by airplane (McCullough, 1992, p. 327)
6. C. South portico of the White House (Burnes, 2003, p. 125)
7. A. "Now, you behave yourself." (Truman, 1955, p. 195)
8. B. 82 days (Leuchtenburg, 2015, p. 246)
9. A. He was the first vice president to be assigned Secret Service protection. (McCullough, 1992, p. 335)
10. D. Many thought that he demeaned the dignity of the office of vice president. (Dorsett, 1996, pp. 16–27).
11. A. In an apartment at 4701 Connecticut Avenue (Brower, 2018, p. 108)
12. A. The one office "in which it is the man who makes the office, not the office the man" (Hamby, 1995, p. 287)
13. A. Suicide of Bess's father (McCullough, 1992, p. 308)
14. D. 1 minute (McCullough, 1992, p. 320)
15. C. "The VP simply presides over the Senate and sits around hoping for a funeral." (McCullough, 1992, pp. 298–299)

Early Presidency

At FDR's funeral in the White House East Room, what presidential courtesy was not afforded HST?

1. Who informed HST that he was president?
   A. Steve Early, FDR's secretary
   B. Eleanor Roosevelt
   C. Sam Rayburn, Speaker of the House
   D. Edward Stettinius, Jr., secretary of state

2. Who predicted that HST would not be as flashy as FDR, "But, by God, he'll make a good president. He's got the stuff in him."
   A. Speaker Sam Rayburn
   B. Congressman Lyndon Johnson
   C. Former Vice President John Nance Gardner
   D. FBI Director J. Edgar Hoover

3. What were some of the first decisions made by HST?
   A. That Mrs. Roosevelt could use an army plane to fly to Georgia and then accompany the president's body back by train to Washington
   B. That the organizational meeting of the United Nations would take place in San Francisco as planned
   C. That the war would end only with unconditional surrender
   D. That he would not run in 1948

4. At FDR's funeral in the White House East Room, what presidential courtesy was not afforded HST?
   A. He was not invited to offer a eulogy.
   B. No one stood when he entered the East Room.
   C. He did not have a reserved seat.
   D. He was not the first to be ushered out at the end of the service.

5. How did HST travel from FDR's funeral train on a siding in Hyde Park to the grave for the committal service?
   A. In the presidential limousine
   B. In an army jeep

C. In a taxi

D. On a chartered bus

6. When HST became president in 1945, what did neighbors in Independence do?

   A. Erected a flagpole in the front yard

   B. Had the Truman home painted a brilliant white

   C. Threw a big barbecue for his first visit home

   D. Had the sidewalks around his house redone and enlarged

7. While HST waited to be sworn in as president, how did one FDR aide describe him?

   A. "A man of distinct limitations."

   B. "A very little man...waiting in a huge leather chair."

   C. "A number-two man suddenly thrust into a number-one job!"

   D. "Too little a man to fill big shoes."

8. How did HST describe his first week as president?

   A. "An hourly struggle to keep my sanity."

   B. "Working in the Oval Office knowing that everyone I saw was thinking, 'the little man is in over his head'!"

   C. "Constantly expecting FDR to say, 'Wasn't that a hell of a trick to pull on the Russians'?"

   D. "I felt as if I had lived five lifetimes in my first five days as president."

9. Who said of HST, "I am very sorry for the president because he is new on the job and he has been brought into a situation which ought not to have been allowed to come his way"?

   A. Henry Stimson, secretary of war

   B. Thomas Dewey, governor of New York

   C. Eleanor Roosevelt

   D. Winston Churchill, prime minister of Great Britain

10. Early in his presidency, while attending the Potsdam Conference, HST was offended when a U.S. Army officer offered what?

   A. A gallon of bourbon for his suite
   B. Intimate female companionship
   C. Discriminatory racial comments
   D. Congratulations for being "a man" in the White House

11. How many reporters showed up for Truman's first press conference on April 17?

   A. 24 reporters
   B. 39 reporters
   C. 112 reporters
   D. 348 reporters

12. What did HST write his brother Vivian about the decisions he faced as president?

   A. "I think, at least once a day, I have the right to tell someone to go to hell."
   B. "I think the proper thing to do, and the thing I have been doing, is to do what I think is right and let them all go to hell."
   C. "It just one damn prima donna after another...."
   D. "I have to listen to people tell me, 'This is what Franklin Roosevelt would do....'"

13. What gave HST nightmares?

   A. Deciding to drop the atomic bomb
   B. Reading reports of displaced persons in Germany
   C. Estimates of potential casualties if the United States invaded Japan
   D. Having to terminate members of FDR's cabinet

14. Why did HST ban Rev. Adam Clayton Powell, Democratic congressman from Harlem, from White House social functions?

A. Powell had publicly insulted Bess as "the Last Lady of the Land."

B. J. Edgar Hoover had informed Truman that Powell was a Communist.

C. Powell pestered HST to appoint an African American to the Supreme Court.

D. Powell jokingly told reporters that Margaret could not even win a blue ribbon at a county fair for her singing.

15. Of what event did HST write his mother, "Wish I didn't have to go, but I do and it can't be stopped"?
   A. Founding meeting of the United Nations in San Francisco
   B. Potsdam Conference with Churchill and Stalin
   C. Funeral of General George C. Marshall
   D. Address to Congress days after FDR's funeral

16. What was HST's early polling number as president?
   A. 58%
   B. 69%
   C. 73%
   D. 87%

17. What action did HST take on his first day in the Oval Office?
   A. Telephoned his mother and said, "Guess where I am calling from?"
   B. Apologized to friends for cancelling the previous night's poker game
   C. Ordered the presidential flag redesigned
   D. Asked for White House safes to be opened for inspection

18. How many hours did HST often work in a day?
   A. 8 hours
   B. 10 hours
   C. 12 hours
   D. 17 hours

19. Why did HST not retain Secretary of State Edward R. Stettinius, Jr.?
    A. Due to then existing presidential succession, in the absence of a vice president, the elderly secretary of state was first in the line of succession.
    B. Stettinius had been appointed by Franklin Roosevelt.
    C. Stettinius was a poor administrator.
    D. Stettinius had said that FDR should have chosen James Byrnes as his running mate in 1944.

20. How did HST assess the responsibility of following FDR into the Oval Office?
    A. "My greatest regret is that we didn't get enough time together."
    B. "Never did I imagine that I could be thrust into this responsibility."
    C. "There have been few men in all history the equal of the man into whose shoes I am stepping."
    D. "I pray that the God who inspired and strengthened Franklin Delano Roosevelt will remember me."

21. Presenting the Medal of Honor challenged HST emotionally. On October 12, 1945, what was unusual about the recognition of the heroism of Pvt. Desmond T. Doss, medical corpsman on Okinawa?
    A. HST's first Medal of Honor awarded to a Missouri resident
    B. First Medal of Honor ever awarded to a conscientious objector
    C. First Medal of Honor given to a son of a Battery D member
    D. First Medal of Honor awarded a double amputee

Early Presidency—*Answers*

1. B. Eleanor Roosevelt (McCullough, 1992, p. 342)
2. A. Speaker Sam Rayburn (Uebelhor, 2006, p. 587)
3. A. That Mrs. Roosevelt could use an army plane to fly to Georgia and then accompany the president's body back by train to Washington. (McCullough, 1992, p. 346)
    B. That the organizational meeting of the United Nations would take place in San Francisco as planned (McCullough, 1992, p. 346)
    C. That the war would end only with unconditional surrender (McCullough, 1992, p. 346)
4. B. No one stood when he entered the East Room. (McCullough, 1992, p. 358)
5. C. In a taxi (Klara, 2010, p. 152)
6. B. Had the Truman home painted a brilliant white (Taylor, 2013, p. 87)
7. B. "A very little man…waiting in a huge leather chair." (Hamby, 1995, p. 294)
8. D. "I felt as if I had lived five lifetimes in my first five days as president." (Whitman, December 27, 1992, p. 46)
9. A. Henry Stimson, secretary of war (McCullough, 1992, p. 375)
10. B. Intimate female companionship (Burnes, 2003, p. 131)
11. D. 348 reporters (Ferrell, 1991, p. 11)
12. B. "I think the proper thing to do, and the thing I have been doing, is to do what I think is right and let them all go to hell." (Ferrell, 1983, p. 84)
13. B. Reading reports of displaced persons in Germany (Independence Productions, 1964)
14. A. Powell had publicly insulted Bess as "the Last Lady of the Land." (McCullough, 1992, p. 576)

15. B. Potsdam Conference with Churchill and Stalin (Truman, 1955, p. 331)

16. D. 87% (Baime, 2017, p. 273)

17. B. Apologized to friends for cancelling the previous night's poker game (Robbins, 1979, p. 98)

18. D. 17 hours (Robbins, 1979, p. 49)

19. A. Due to then existing presidential succession, in the absence of a vice president, the elderly secretary of state was first in the line of succession. (Ferrell, 1983, p. 67)

20. C. "There have been few men in all history the equal of the man into whose shoes I am stepping." (Lepore, 2018, p. 511)

21. B. The first medal of honor ever awarded to a conscientious objector (Doss)

World War II

Because of the Russian belligerence in Berlin and across Europe, how did HST blast the former allies?

1. When Senator Truman, age 56, tried to volunteer for the U.S. Army in World War II, what did General Marshall tell him?
   A. "You're serving the military well on the Truman Committee."
   B. "This war will be fought by young men."
   C. "Sir, you can best serve your country in the U.S. Senate!"
   D. "You're too damn old!"

2. As a Senator in 1941, before Pearl Harbor, what did HST say about the combatants, Germany and Russia?
   A. "It doesn't take a genius to figure out whose side we should be on."
   B. "It's just another European dust-up that does not concern us. Yet!"
   C. "We can just wait for Darwin's survival of the fittest."
   D. "If we see that Germany is winning the war, we ought to help Russia; and if Russia is winning, we ought to help Germany, and in that way let them kill as many as possible...."

3. When did the Joint Chiefs project World War II might end?
   A. November 1945
   B. November 1946
   C. February 1947
   D. Uncertain

4. How did Stalin assess HST before meeting him?
   A. "A country bumpkin"
   B. "Always expected the worse from him"
   C. "Prejudiced against Russia"
   D. "A poor excuse to follow Roosevelt"

5. At Potsdam, HST soon realized his powerlessness to change Russia's position on what?

A. Post-war boundaries of Poland
B. Resentment over the abrupt termination of Lend-Lease
C. Public execution of Nazi war criminals
D. Cooperation in administering liberated areas of Eastern Europe

6. Because of the Russian belligerence in Berlin and across Europe, how did HST blast the former allies?
A. "Resentful bastards of the first order"
B. "World class thieves"
C. "Natural looters"
D. "Liars, rapists, bandits"

7. When HST sent Harry Hopkins to Moscow to assess the strained relations between the two superpowers, he authorized him to use "diplomatic language" or what?
A. A baseball bat
B. A checkbook
C. Kiss Stalin's ass in Red Square
D. Promise to resume Lend-Lease shipments

8. When Russian Ambassador Vyacheslav Molotov met HST in the Oval Office, the president ripped into him. Finally, Molotov blustered, "I have never been talked to like that in my life...." How did HST respond?
A. "Mr. Ambassador, there is an old American expression: 'There's a new sheriff in town!' Well, sir, that new sheriff is me!"
B. "Well, get this straight: You are not going to pull the damn tricks and shenanigans you pulled with my predecessor! Do I make myself clear?"
C. "Carry out your agreements and you won't get talked to like that."
D. "Take Mr. Stalin a message from me: Harry Truman can be one mean son of a bitch when I need to be."

9. HST doubted Russia's willingness to keep the promises it made to the allies. Agreements made at Potsdam, from HST's point of view, were broken when?

   A. "While that ole bastard was shaking my hand goodbye."
   B. "Before Stalin's eastbound train reached full speed."
   C. "Before that lying bastard's ass left his chair."
   D. "As soon as the unconscionable Russian dictator reached the Moscow city limits."

10. Where did HST insist the Japanese surrender?

    A. On board the USS *Missouri* anchored in Tokyo harbor
    B. In Hirohito's palace in Tokyo
    C. A safe spot in Hiroshima
    D. MacArthur's offices at the Dai-ichi Life Insurance Company in Tokyo

11. For an 11:00 a.m. meeting, who did Truman force to get up earlier than he had in decades?

    A. Clement Attlee
    B. Josef Stalin
    C. Edward R. Stettinius, Jr.
    D. Winston Churchill

12. When the war in Europe ended, what did HST write his mother about his priorities?

    A. "To make a peace that will last for generations"
    B. "We have another war to win."
    C. "To get our boys home to their wives, sweethearts, and mamas"
    D. "To build an economy that will be generous to our veterans who have sacrificed so much"

13. Instead of the anticipated "peace dividend" following World War II, HST had to confront what?

    A. Containment of communism
    B. Unprecedented peacetime military spending
    C. A new military bureaucracy

D. Controversy over plans to eliminate the Marine Corps

14. What did HST consistently say about his decision to drop atomic bombs?
    A. "It had to be done. Period."
    B. "I have been asked whether I have any regrets about any of the major decisions I had to make as president. I have none."
    C. "I got the best advice from the wisest men I could."
    D. "There are always professors and retired generals sitting around wasting time second-guessing a president's decisions."

15. After two atomic bombs were dropped, Samuel Mc-Crea Cavert, general secretary of a national church group, chastised HST for the decision. How did HST respond?
    A. "Nobody is more disturbed over the use of the atomic bombs than I am.... When you have to deal with a beast you have to treat him as a beast."
    B. "Reverend, have you ever heard of 'the separation of church and state'? Apparently not, judging from your letter."
    C. "I wish I had had other options but the emperor left me no choice."
    D. "If we had invaded Japan, many young soldiers would not have come home and made babies to fill your Sunday school classes."

16. How did Stalin respond, at Potsdam, when HST reported that the United States had tested a new bomb of "extraordinary destructive power"?
    A. Showed very little interest
    B. Ordered the Soviet atomic energy program to accelerate its work
    C. Questioned why a new bomb was needed when the war was almost won
    D. Demanded a detailed scientific explanation

17. Why was HST reluctant to tell Stalin about the A-bomb?
    A. Did not want to disclose the nature of the bomb
    B. Feared that Stalin would want Russians to observe future tests
    C. Feared that Stalin would be angry for being kept in the dark by Truman and Churchill
    D. Feared that the Russians would think the war was won and not engage Japan

18. Two decades after his decision, how did HST defend his decision to use the atomic bomb?
    A. "The Japanese gave this commander-in-chief no other options to end the war."
    B. "I made that decision in the conviction that it would save hundreds of thousands of lives, Japanese as well as Americans."
    C. "I saved tens of thousands of young boys and gave them futures."
    D. "On that particular day in August 1945, 'the buck stopped' on my desk."

19. What greatly contributed to the second-guessing of HST's decision to use the bomb?
    A. Albert Einstein's letter of protest
    B. Churchill's silence on HST's decision
    C. John Hershey's graphic description of the devastation in his magazine article "Hiroshima"
    D. Reports that the bombs were unnecessary because the emperor had been ready to abdicate

20. Who later claimed to have disagreed with HST's use of the bomb?
    A. General Dwight Eisenhower
    B. General George Marshall
    C. Prime Minister Clement Atlee
    D. Henry Stimson, secretary of war

21. What did almost one in four Americans believe about the bomb?
    A. Should have been used earlier
    B. The United States should have dropped "many more" atomic bombs on Japan before the surrender
    C. Should have been dropped on Germany
    D. Should *never* have been used!

22. Once the Russians developed the bomb, what did HST feel compelled to do?
    A. Develop more powerful atomic bombs
    B. Begin research on a hydrogen bomb
    C. Consider launching a preemptive strike on Russian bomb factories
    D. Negotiate with Stalin for both nations to stop producing bombs

World War II—*Answers*

1. D. "You're too damn old!" (Truman, 1973, p. 148)
2. D. "If we see that Germany is winning the war, we ought to help Russia; and if Russia is winning, we ought to help Germany, and in that way let them kill as many as possible...." (Hamby, 1995, p. 270)
3. B. November 1946 (Hedley, 1979, p. 97)
4. B. "Always expected the worse from him" (Steil, 2018, p. 5)
5. D. Cooperation in administering liberated areas of Eastern Europe (Hedley, 1979, p. 86)
6. C. "Natural looters" (Timberlake, 1989, p. 339)
7. A. A baseball bat (Truman, 1973, p. 252)
8. C. "Carry out your agreements and you won't get talked to like that." (Ferrell, 1983, p. 50)
9. D. "As soon as the unconscionable Russian dictator reached the Moscow city limits" (Robbins, 1979, p. 108; Truman at Potsdam, June/July 1980)
10. A. On board the USS *Missouri* anchored in Tokyo harbor (Matuz, 2004, p. 540)
11. D. Winston Churchill (Ferrell, 1983, p. 52)
12. B. "We have another war to win." (Truman, 1973, p. 243)
13. A. Containment of communism (Lepore, 2018, p. 538)
    B. Unprecedented peacetime military spending (Lepore, 2018, p. 538)
    C. A new military bureaucracy (Lepore, 2018, p. 538)
14. B. "I have been asked whether I have any regrets about any of the major decisions I had to make as president. I have none." (Truman, 1953, p. 262)
15. A. "Nobody is more disturbed over the use of the atomic bomb than I am.... When you have to deal with a beast you have to treat him as a beast." (Wyden, 1985, p. 294)

16. A. Showed very little interest (Ferrell, 1983, p. 53)
17. A. Did not want to disclose the nature of the bomb (History.com, June 7, 2019)
18. B. "I made that decision in the conviction that it would save hundreds of thousands of lives, Japanese as well as Americans." (Williams, August 6, 2005)
19. C. John Hershey's graphic description of the devastation in his magazine article "Hiroshima" (Hershey, 1946, pp. 15–26)
20. A. General Dwight Eisenhower (Eisenhower, 1963)
21. B. The United States should have dropped "many more" atomic bombs on Japan before the surrender (Walker, 1997, p. 98)
22. B. Begin research on a hydrogen bomb (Hamby, 1995, p. 525)

President

Who persuaded HST to erect an iron fence around his home in Independence to protect against souvenir seekers?

1. What event on October 1, 1949, significantly challenged HST's foreign policy and relationship with Congress?
   A. General George C. Marshall died
   B. Mao proclaimed the People's Republic of China
   C. Russia detonated an atomic devise
   D. China and Russia signed a mutual aid pact

2. Who, over time, became HST's most influential adviser on foreign affairs?
   A. Dean Acheson
   B. George C. Marshall
   C. Arthur H. Vandenberg
   D. Clark Clifford

3. Who persuaded HST to erect an iron fence around his home in Independence to protect against souvenir seekers?
   A. Roger T. Sermon, mayor of Independence
   B. Herbert Hoover, former president
   C. Eddie Jacobson, his longtime friend
   D. The Secret Service

4. Who did HST concede would have made a better president?
   A. General Dwight Eisenhower
   B. A million other men
   C. General Douglas MacArthur
   D. Senator Robert Taft of Ohio

5. What did Truman often call visitors to the Oval Office?
   A. "The people"
   B. "Customers"
   C. "Eye-ballers"
   D. "The president's clients"

6. HST was loudly booed at what event in 1951?
   A. AFL-CIO National Convention
   B. California State Democratic Convention
   C. When he threw out the first pitch of the baseball season in Washington, DC
   D. San Francisco crowds welcoming MacArthur home

7. What president did HST identify as his favorite?
   A. George Washington
   B. Woodrow Wilson
   C. Franklin D. Roosevelt
   D. Andrew Jackson

8. Why did HST have little use for Franklin Roosevelt's sons?
   A. They actively supported Ike for president in 1948.
   B. They thought the Democratic party owed them "a fast track" to pursue their political careers.
   C. "All Roosevelts want the personal aggrandizement...."
   D. Their mother coddled them.

9. What was unique about HST's inauguration in 1949?
   A. First inaugural to be televised
   B. He had an "enormous appropriation" to spend for the festivities because the Republicans expected to win in 1948.
   C. The vice president took the oath of office in a hospital bed.
   D. Washington, DC, experienced a record high temperature.

10. HST was the first president to address what organization?
   A. U.S. Catholic Conference of Bishops
   B. Daughters of the American Revolution
   C. The NAACP
   D. National Rifle Association

11. Why did HST dislike J. Edgar Hoover, head of the FBI?
    A. Hoover did not follow proper channels in communicating with the White House.
    B. Hoover leaked information to conservative politicians.
    C. Hoover insinuated that the Truman administration was indifferent to the growing Communist threat.
    D. Hoover peddled salacious material on politicians.

12. Why did HST rarely use Shangri-La, the presidential retreat in Maryland now known as Camp David?
    A. It required an inconvenient drive from the White House.
    B. The flora aggravated his allergies.
    C. Margaret thought the place "terrible," cold and damp "most of the time."
    D. It was located in a "dry" county.

13. What was HSTs domestic legislative program called?
    A. The Fair Deal
    B. The Victory Deal
    C. The Patriot Deal
    D. The American Deal

14. What presidential perk did HST most enjoy?
    A. Speeding through traffic lights
    B. The presidential yacht, the USS *Williamsburg*
    C. The service by Filipino stewards
    D. People standing when he entered the room

15. When Margaret and Bess went home to Independence for extended periods of time, what did HST call the White House?
    A. "The loneliest residence in Washington"
    B. "A rich man's jail"
    C. "A charmless, rundown hotel"
    D. "The great white prison"

16. How were the shooters who attempted to assassinate HST described?
    A. Russian separatists
    B. Puerto Rican freedom fighters
    C. Ku Klux Klan members
    D. Communist Chinese agents

17. Immediately following the assassination attempt, what did Press Secretary Charlie Ross tell reporters?
    A. "Such things are to be expected."
    B. "I've never seen a calmer man."
    C. "Good thing the Secret Service got to the assassins first; otherwise, Harry would have beaten the hell out of them."
    D. "Harry will need a double bourbon tonight."

18. Where did HST go one hour after the assassination attempt?
    A. To a ceremony at Arlington National Cemetery
    B. To a meeting in Speaker Sam Rayburn's office
    C. To pray in Saint John's Episcopal Church near the White House
    D. To play poker at the Willard Hotel

19. Why did HST agree to new Secret Service guidelines that restricted his walks and movements outdoors?
    A. "I had to acknowledge that if a wacko took a shot at me, innocent bystanders might be injured."
    B. "Someone has to be able to say: 'No, Mr. President, you cannot do that.'"
    C. "I want no more guards killed."
    D. "The Boss sided with the Secret Service."

20. How did HST describe the presidency?
    A. "An impossible administrative burden"
    B. "The greatest responsibility that has ever fallen to a human being"
    C. "A five-ulcer job" most days
    D. "A glass fishbowl full of hungry sharks"

21. What organization did HST actively participate in as president and as a former president?
   A. Americans for Democratic Action
   B. The American Legion
   C. The Masonic Lodge
   D. American Farm Bureau

22. As president, HST formed a close friendship with what well-known Republican?
   A. Senator Joseph McCarthy
   B. Former president Herbert Hoover
   C. Senator Robert Taft
   D. Governor Thomas Dewey

23. What did Truman write to his daughter about his presidency?
   A. "I made a hell of a better president than Ike!"
   B. "Your pop did his damnedest to make life better for every American."
   C. "Your dad will never be reckoned among the great."
   D. "Your pop never quit no matter what those damn Republicans said or did."

24. Who called HST, "Truman the Human"?
   A. General Harry Vaughn
   B. News correspondents
   C. White House resident staff
   D. The Secret Service

25. How did HST announce it was time for to play poker?
   A. "I think we've done given the government our best for one day."
   B. "Who's ready to win a little money?"
   C. "It must be time for a little paperwork."
   D. "And now, let's get to the day's most important business."

26. As president, how many words did HST read a day?
    A. 10,000
    B. 20,000
    C. 30,000
    D. "As many words as needed to be read"

27. What activity did HST particularly enjoy in Key West?
    A. Getting behind the steering wheel of a big convertible and cruising along city streets and out on the highway along the Atlantic
    B. Interacting with tourists
    C. Deep-sea fishing
    D. Relaxing on the beach

28. How much did Harry Truman's first Oval Office television set cost?
    A. $375
    B. $512
    C. $1,795
    D. Nothing. General Electric donated it.

29. HST created a storm of controversy by proposing to appoint an ambassador to what nation?
    A. Communist China
    B. The Vatican
    C. Poland
    D. Hungary

30. How many resolutions of impeachment against Truman were filed in the House of Representatives in 1952?
    A. 0
    B. 5
    C. 14
    D. 17

31. In 1952, what was HST's major beef with General Eisenhower?

A. Ike had failed to defend the reputation of his mentor George Marshall.
B. Ike was idolized by the American public.
C. Ike had never voted.
D. Ike was backed by wealthy businessmen.

32. Who did HST most want to succeed him in 1953?
A. Fred Vinson
B. Adlai Stevenson
C. Estes Kefauver
D. William O. Douglas

33. What did HST believe about the 1952 presidential election?
A. He could win another term as president
B. Eisenhower would trounce Adlai Stevenson
C. A high percentage of Americans would not vote
D. General Eisenhower was beatable

34. Truman described what cabinet member as "the worst egomaniac I've ever come in contact with—and I've seen a lot."
A. Henry Morgenthau, secretary of the treasury
B. Lewis Johnson, secretary of defense
C. James Byrnes, Jr., secretary of state
D. Thomas Clark, attorney general

35. Who did HST say was "the worst" appointment he made as president?
A. James Byrnes as secretary of state
B. Frederick Vinson as chief justice, U.S. Supreme Court
C. Thomas C. Clark to the U.S. Supreme Court
D. J. Howard McGrath as attorney general

36. According to Margaret Truman, what warning did HST give his aides?
    A. "Keep your eyes open and your mouth shut."
    B. "If your mouth is open it had better be because I just asked you a question."
    C. "I hired you for your eyes and ears—*not* for your mouth."
    D. "Gentlemen, this is the way it works around here: From my mouth to your ears."

37. Who made the sign on HST's desk, "The Buck Stops Here"?
    A. Sailors on the USS *Missouri*
    B. Prisoners in the Federal Reformatory at El Reno, Oklahoma
    C. Autoworkers in Detroit
    D. Woodworkers on the White House staff

38. On a trip home, HST visited Eddie Jacobson's new haberdashery to buy a shirt. A chagrinned Jacobson admitted that he did not have a dress white shirt in Harry's size (15½, 33). What happened after newspapers reported the incident?
    A. Several reporters sent him "the shirt off our backs."
    B. Bess scolded him, "You embarrassed Eddie. You should have let him know you were coming!"
    C. Admirers sent some 2,000 white shirts to Truman.
    D. Eddie Jacobson started giving reporters big discounts on their purchases.

39. Which press secretaries died during HST's administration?
    A. Charles S. Murphy
    B. Charlie Ross
    C. Steven Early
    D. Joseph H. Short

40. During a potentially crippling railroad strike in

May 1946, what did HST say to intimidate two obstinate union leaders?

A. "Let me guess—neither of you have ever dealt with a Missouri mule, have you?"
B. "If you think I'm going to sit here and let you tie up the whole country, you're crazy as hell!"
C. "How did such dumb asses get to be union leaders?"
D. "Have you considered what would happen to you if you tried this with Josef Stalin?"

41. What was HST's topic for the first presidential address ever televised from the White House on October 5, 1947?

A. Food conservation and the world food crisis
B. The need to consolidate the military
C. Authorizing the United Nations to control atomic energy
D. Why the United Nations headquarters should be built in New York City

42. How did HST explain where the responsibilities of the president take place?

A. "Wherever I happened to be, that's where the Office of the President was."
B. "Sometimes on the *Williamsburg*"
C. "Always in the White House"
D. "On my plane"

43. What did HST call the original United Nations charter signed in San Francisco in 1945?

A. "A once-in-a-millennia moment to do the right thing for the rights of all mankind"
B. "A victory against war itself"
C. "A chance to create an enduring peace under the guidance of God"
D. "The Declaration of Independence for the whole world"

44. The commitment of the United States to "support free peoples who are restricting subjugation by armed minorities or by outside pressures" was called what?

A. The Fair Deal
B. The Global Democracy Initiative
C. The Truman Doctrine
D. The Marshall Plan

45. Although he had said he would not run for another term in 1952, HST was tempted to reconsider in order to do what?

A. To push for universal health care
B. To validate his decisions in Korea
C. To keep the Democrats from "going off the rails"
D. To finish the work of his Fair Deal

46. The American Medical Association spent $5 million to defeat HST's proposal for what innovation?

A. National health insurance plan
B. Expansion of National Institute of Health
C. Creation of the military's own medical school
D. Expansion of Social Security for drug costs

47. The White House physician was sworn to secrecy to hide what medical condition of HST from the American public?

A. Atrial fibrillation
B. Cardiac asthma
C. Congestive heart disease
D. Sinus tachycardia

48. How did HST dispel rumors of ghosts in the White House?

A. "I suspect the only ghost in this house is the Holy Ghost."

B. "Just something some of the staff joke about"
C. "About as likely as a Wall Street banker sleeping in the Lincoln Bedroom!"
D. "Damn place is haunted sure as shootin'."

49. What were HST's worst fears about the physical condition of the White House?
    A. Fire
    B. Collapse
    C. Congressional Republicans would claim it cheaper to build a *new* presidential residence
    D. Foundation was crumbling from age

50. Where was HST when chandeliers in the East Room began to jingle during Bess's reception for DAR members?
    A. Upstairs taking an afternoon nap
    B. Upstairs editing a speech
    C. Upstairs taking a bath
    D. Marching in place because he could not take his daily walk in the rain

51. What was one unexpected complication in the rebuilding of the White House?
    A. Lack of skilled artists to duplicate damaged moldings
    B. Prices of construction materials soared dramatically because of the Korean War.
    C. Discovery in basement walls of buried chests filled with White House silverware hidden before the British burned the White House in 1814
    D. Discovery of three graves in the basement

52. HST made certain that the restoration of the White House came in under budget? How much money was spent on the project?
   A. $1.5 million and all the money Truman could personally raise from wealthy donors
   B. $3.75 million
   C. $5.8 million
   D. $7 million total

53. After the rebuilding was completed, how did HST assess the investment?
   A. "It will last long into my grandchildren's grandchildren's day!"
   B. "The sturdy rebuilt White House will stand for centuries."
   C. "It could easily have cost twice as much."
   D. "A facility that outshines Buckingham Palace, the Taj Mahal, and Versailles, for that matter."

54. In a ceremony to formally welcome HST back to the White House, what object was presented to the president?
   A. A gold-plated mason's trowel
   B. A first-floor plan printed on ancient Chinese paper
   C. A gold door key
   D. A bust of Andrew Jackson carved out of recycled White House marble

55. What did HST do with some of the original stones from the White House walls?
   A. Had them set into the White House kitchen walls
   B. Sent stones to the Masonic grand lodges
   C. Had them made into a walking path in the Rose Garden
   D. Donated to the Smithsonian Institution

56. During the renovation, upon discovering that the Russians had detonated an atomic bomb, what ma-

jor adjustment was made to the architectural plans?

A. More steel was added to the internal framework.
B. The basement was deepened for a hermetically sealed bunker capable of withstanding a nuclear blast.
C. Triple-thick panes of glass were installed.
D. A gigantic generator was added.

57. What did HST *do* before 30 million Americans during the first-ever televised tour of the renovated White House in May 1952?

A. Played two grand pianos in the East Room
B. Showed viewers the president's private bathroom
C. Nibbled cookie dough in the new kitchen
D. Asked the host if he would like to come back later and play some poker

58. In 1952, HST broke tradition and asked President-elect Dwight Eisenhower to meet with him to work on what?

A. Clearing the air about some campaign rhetoric
B. Ensuring an orderly transfer of the office
C. Requisitioning resources for Eisenhower's trip to Korea
D. Change in the military command in Korea

President—*Answers*

1. B. Mao proclaimed the People's Republic of China (Peraino, 2017, pp. 211–212)
2. A. Dean Acheson (Hamby, 1995, p. 510)
3. B. Herbert Hoover, former president (Truman, 1973, p. 560)
4. B. A million other men (Truman, 1989, p. 1)
5. B. "Customers" (Hamby, 1995, p. 468)
6. C. When he threw out the first pitch of the baseball season in Washington, DC (Matuz, 2004, p. 547)
7. D. Andrew Jackson (Mancini, March 1, 2016; Truman, 1989, p. 272)
8. C. "All Roosevelts want the personal aggrandizement...." (Beschloss, 2007, p. 213)
9. B. He had an "enormous appropriation" to spend for the festivities because the Republicans expected to win in 1948. (Ferrell, 1983, p. 104)
10. C. The NAACP (Zangrando, 1989, p. 250)
11. A. Hoover did not follow proper channels in communicating with the White House. (Theoharis, 1989, p. 161)
    B. Hoover leaked information to conservative politicians. (Theoharis, 1989, p. 161)
    C. Hoover insinuated that the Truman administration was indifferent to the growing Communist threat. (Theoharis, 1989, p. 161)
    D. Hoover peddled salacious material on politicians. (Theoharis, 1989, p. 161)
12. C. Margaret thought the place "terrible," cold and damp "most of the time." (Truman, 1973, p. 334)
13. A. The Fair Deal (Yates, 1989, p. 123)
14. B. The presidential yacht, the USS *Williamsburg* (Yates, 1989, p. 388)
15. D. "The great white prison" (McCoy, 1989, p. 285)

16. B. Puerto Rican freedom fighters (Troy, 1989, p. 13)
17. B. "I've never seen a calmer man." (Healy, December 2, 1950, np)
18. A. To a ceremony at Arlington National Cemetery (Truman, 1973, p. 488)
19. C. "I want no more guards killed." (Ferrell, 1980, p. 198)
20. B. "The greatest responsibility that has ever fallen to a human being" (McCoy, 1989, p. 285)
21. C. The Masonic Lodge (Roberts, 2012, p. xi)
22. B. Former president Herbert Hoover (Best, 1989, p. 159)
23. C. "Your dad will never be reckoned among the great." (McCoy, 1989, p. 287)
24. B. News correspondents (Walsh, 2005, p. 121)
25. C. "It must be time for a little paperwork." (Walsh, 2005, p. 117)
26. C. 30,000 (Curtis, 1989, p. 295)
27. A. Getting behind the steering wheel of a big convertible and cruising along city streets and out on the highway along the Atlantic (Walsh, 2005, p. 117)
28. C. $1,795 (Algeo, 2009, p. 157)
29. B. The Vatican (Kirkendall, 2008, p. 222)
30. C. 14 (Pemberton, 1989, p. 158)
31. A. Ike had failed to defend the reputation of his mentor George Marshall. (Ambrose, 1989, p. 109)
32. A. Fred Vinson (Truman, 1973, p. 527; Barnes, 2006, p. 617)
33. A. He could win another term as president (Ferrell, 1980, p. 178)
34. B. Lewis Johnson, secretary of defense (Robbins, 1979, p. 118)
35. C. Thomas C. Clark to the U.S. Supreme Court (Pemberton, 1989, p. 149)
36. A. "Keep your eyes open and your mouth shut." (Truman, 2004, p. 169)

37. B. Prisoners in the Federal Reformatory at El Reno, Oklahoma (https://www.trumanlibrary.gov/educa tion.trivia/buck-stops-here sign)

38. C. Admirers sent some 2,000 white shirts to Truman. (Truman, 2004, p. 388)

39. B. Charlie Ross (Pemberton, 1989, p. 148)

   D. Joseph H. Short (Pemberton, 1989, p. 148)

40. B. "If you think I'm going to sit here and let you tie up the whole country, you're crazy as hell!" (Ferrell, 1983, p. 91)

41. A. Food conservation and the world food crisis (Kane & Podell, 2009, p. 409)

42. A. "Wherever I happened to be, that's where the Office of the President was." (Knutson, 2014, p. 256)

43. B. "A victory against war itself." (Lepore, 2018, p. 512)

   C. "A chance to create an enduring peace under the guidance of God." (Lepore, 2018, p. 513)

44. C. The Truman Doctrine (Lepore, 2018, p. 537)

45. B. To validate his decisions in Korea (Beschloss, 2018, p. 474)

46. A. National health insurance plan (Lepore, 2018, p. 548)

47. B. Cardiac asthma (Beschloss, 2018, p. 477)

48. D. "Damn place is haunted sure as shootin'." (Truman, 2004, p. 12)

49. B. Collapse (Seale, 2008, p. 1026)

50. C. Upstairs taking a bath (Klara, 2013, p. 6)

51. B. Prices of construction materials soared dramatically because of the Korean War. (Seale, 2008, p. 1039)

52. C. $5.8 million (Brandus, 2015, p. 195)

53. B. "The sturdy rebuilt White House will stand for centuries." (Robbins, 1979, p. 110)

54. C. A gold door key (Seale, 2008, p. 1051)

55. A. Had them set into the White House kitchen walls (Seale, 2008, p. 1038)

    B. Sent stones to the Masonic grand lodges (Seale, 2008, p. 1038)

56. B. The basement was deepened for a hermetically sealed bunker capable of withstanding a nuclear blast. (Sides, 2018, p. 91)

57. A. Played two grand pianos in the East Room (McCullough, 1992, p. 886)

58. B. Ensuring an orderly transfer of the office (Hedley, 1979, p. 291)

Defining Global Responsibility

What did HST regard as "the toughest" and "most important" decision in his presidency?

1. In early 1947, HST asked Congress to fund billions for aid for Turkey and Greece, to contain Russia's expansion and to give Western Europe a chance to stabilize from the war. What was this policy called?
   A. The European Defense Initiative
   B. NATO
   C. The Truman Doctrine
   D. The Marshall Plan

2. HST proposed offering funds to nations to restructure their postwar economies. What was this program called?
   A. The Good Neighbor Policy
   B. The Truman Aid Initiative
   C. The Marshall Plan
   D. The Fair Deal

3. HST linked the military security of Europe and the United States through what provision in the NATO treaty?
   A. That an attack on one member would be considered an attack on all members
   B. For the first five years the United States would match what the other nations invested into the organization
   C. The United States would never force its desires upon other member nations
   D. The United States would not act against the formation of a united Europe

4. HST described the Truman Doctrine and the Marshall Plan as what?
   A. "Two peas in a pod"
   B. "Two halves of the same walnut"
   C. "The yin and yang"
   D. "The salt and pepper of foreign policy"

5. What syndicated columnist defended General MacArthur and blasted HST for not standing up to the Russians in Eastern Europe.
   A. Lowell Thomas
   B. Drew Pearson
   C. Westbrook Pegler
   D. Walter Winchell

6. What actions did HST authorize in Germany aware that the Russians might respond with force?
   A. Merged the French, American, and British zones
   B. Implemented currency reform
   C. Expanded German industry
   D. Established self-regulatory institutions

7. Members of Congress objected to which of the following aspects of the Marshall Plan?
   A. Violated Thomas Jefferson's warnings about "entangling alliances"
   B. Would annoy the Russians
   C. Would draw the United States into conflicts between sovereign European nations
   D. Could challenge the U.S. domestic spending

8. What was the projected cost of the Marshall Plan?
   A. $835 million
   B. $2 billion
   C. $7.8 billion
   D. $13 billion

9. When the Russians denied the Allies access to Berlin, HST authorized a massive program for supplying the needs of Berliners for over a year. What was this plan named?
   A. "Blockade Busters"
   B. "Operation 'I Dare You!'"
   C. "Berlin Airlift"
   D. "The Rebuilding European Economies Act"

10. What two intelligence agencies did HST create?
    A. Central Intelligence Agency
    B. National Security Council
    C. Joint Chiefs of Staff Intelligence Command
    D. U.S. Intelligence Administration

11. What did HST regard as "the toughest" and "most important" decision in his presidency?
    A. Using atomic bombs twice
    B. Intervening in Korea
    C. Firing General MacArthur
    D. Withstanding the pressure from Democratic "big dogs" to step aside in 1948

Defining Global Responsibility—*Answers*

1. C. The Truman Doctrine (Beschloss, 2000, p. 397)
2. C. The Marshall Plan (Beschloss, 2000, p. 397)
3. A. That an attack on one member would be considered an attack on all members (Kaplan, 1989, p. 258)
4. B. "Two halves of the same walnut" (Lepore, 2018, p. 538)
5. D. Walter Winchell (Uebelhor, 2006, p. 649)
6. A. Merged the French, American, and British zones (Leffler, 1992, p. 218)

    B. Implemented currency reform (Leffler, 1992, p. 218)

    C. Expanded German industry (Leffler, 1992, p. 218)

    D. Established self-regulatory institutions (Leffler, 1992, p. 218)
7. A. Violated Thomas Jefferson's warnings about "entangling alliances" (Ferrell, 1983, p. 65)

    B. Would annoy the Russians (Ferrell, 1983, p. 65)

    C. Would draw the United States into conflicts between sovereign European nations (Ferrell, 1983, p. 65)

    D. Could challenge the U.S. domestic spending (Ferrell, 1983, p. 65)
8. D. $13 billion (Weisbrode, 2016, p. 205)
9. C. "Berlin Airlift" (Hedley, 1979, pp. 147–150)
10. A. Central Intelligence Agency (Pemberton, 1989, p. 152)

    B. National Security Council (Pemberton, 1989, p. 152)
11. B. Intervening in Korea (Pemberton, 1989, p. 135)

Recognizing the State of Israel

HST recognized the State of Israel against whose advice?

1. In one meeting after arguments between staff became intense about the pros and cons of recognizing Israel, HST stood and said what?
   A. "How in the hell am I supposed to make a decision if you gentlemen cannot agree?"
   B. "Oh, hell, I'm leaving."
   C. "Gentlemen, it all comes down to this: oil!"
   D. "I am damned if I do and damned if I don't!"

2. What friend did HST playfully call a "bald-headed son of a bitch" for lobbying him so zealously to recognize the State of Israel?
   A. Rabbi Steven Wise
   B. Henry Morgenthau
   C. Eddie Jacobson
   D. Joseph M. Proskauer

3. What biblical character did HST call himself for recognizing Israel?
   A. Moses
   B. Abraham
   C. Cyrus
   D. Nehemiah

4. After carefully studying the story of the hope of a "Jewish homeland," HST became skeptical of what?
   A. Attitudes of the "striped-pants boys" in the State Department
   B. What FDR would have done
   C. "The inability of the Jews to defend themselves against the Arabs"
   D. "The potential for igniting a third world war"

5. In a moment of great frustration dealing with the Jews and Zionists, what did HST exclaim?
   A. "Jesus Christ couldn't please them when he was here on earth, so how could anyone expect that I would have any luck?"

B. "It would have been easier to reason with some of my mules on the farm in Grandview."

C. "Just once I wish they would say, 'Damn, aren't we lucky ole Harry is in the White House!'"

D. "I understand why some people become anti-Semitic."

6. What was most influential in HST's recognition of the State of Israel?

A. His friendship with Eddie Jacobson

B. His reading of ancient history and the Bible

C. His desire to increase his Jewish vote in 1948

D. His anger at British incompetence in administering Palestine

7. HST recognized the State of Israel against whose advice?

A. Vice President Alben Barkley

B. The State Department

C. Supreme Court Justice Felix Frankfurter

D. The Senate Foreign Relations Committee

8. When, Yitzchak Herzog, the chief rabbi of Israel, visited the Oval Office one year after the recognition, what did he say that caused HST to cry?

A. "You, sir, like Esther, have come to this moment, 'for such a time as this.'"

B. "You were placed in your mother's womb to give the Jewish people a homeland."

C. "You listened to Jehovah rather than all the wise men around you."

D. "There are less than a handful of politicians who have as much political courage as you."

9. How did HST defend his decision on Israel: "I felt that Israel deserved to be recognized" and what?

    A. "[I] didn't give a damn whether the Arabs liked it or not."
    B. "I would have made the same decision even if the Wallace-ites in the Democratic party denied me the nomination in 1948."
    C. "I had to beat the Russians to the punch."
    D. "I would have done the same thing even if not one more Jew voted for me in the fall."

10. How did HST defend his decision to recognize Israel—against the intense advice of the State Department?"

    A. "I wanted it known that General Marshall and I could disagree strongly and still work together."
    B. "I wanted to make it plain that the president... was responsible for making policy."
    C. "I wanted it understood that even the second and third echelons in the State Department took their marching orders from *me!*"
    D. "I wanted to show the world who was boss!"

11. As HST prepared to leave the White House, what did he say to the National Jewish Welfare Board on his recognition of Israel's right to exist?

    A. "I am proud of my part in the creation of this new state."
    B. "My mama believed this day would come but never that her son would be the decider!"
    C. "Don't ever forget this: If there had been a Republican in the Oval Office they would have listened to the oil boys and kicked the can down the road!"
    D. "That day 'the buck' dropped on my desk with a thud!"

12. In honor of HST's strong support for the independent State of Israel, what honor was bestowed on him?

A. Named an "honorary rabbi"
B. Named an honorary citizen of Israel
C. Library in largest temple in Miami was renamed for Truman
D. Created a large scholarship fund to honor Truman

13. What future Israeli leader, then a soldier/student, sat and talked with HST in the kitchen at 219 N. Delaware?
A. David Ben-Gurion
B. Yitzhak Rabin
C. Moshe Dayan
D. Menachem Begin

Recognizing the State of Israel—*Answers*

1. B. "Oh, hell, I'm leaving." (Beschloss, 2007, p. 209)
2. C. Eddie Jacobson (McCullough, 1992, p. 607)
3. C. Cyrus (Beschloss, 2007, p. 234; Merkley, 2004, p. vii)
4. A. Attitudes of the "striped-pants boys" in the State Department (Hamby, 1995, pp. 408–409)
5. A. "Jesus Christ couldn't please them when he was here on earth, so how could anyone expect that I would have any luck?" (Pemberton, 1989, p. 120)
6. B. His reading of ancient history and the Bible (McCullough, 1992, p. 597; Merkley, 2008, p. 30)
7. B. The State Department (Hamby, 1995, pp. 408–409)
8. B. "You were placed in your mother's womb to give the Jewish people a homeland." (Holmes, 2012, p. 16)
9. A. "[I] didn't give a damn whether the Arabs liked it or not." (Truman, 1989, p. 64)
10. B. "I wanted to make plain that the president...is responsible for making policy." (Leuchtenburg, 2015, p. 281)
11. A. "I am proud of my part in the creation of this new state." (Truman, October 17, 1952)
12. A. Named an "honorary rabbi" (Wolz & Hayo, 2012, p. 150)
13. C. Moshe Dayan (Daniels, September 20, 2017, personal interview)

Election of 1948

In 1948, what member of Congress, in a blistering attack at the Republican National Convention, called HST "a man of phlegm, not of fire."

1. What did HST say about seeking the Democratic presidential nomination in 1948?
   A. "Any shithead behind this desk can get renominated."
   B. "There's no way the convention would deny me the nomination!"
   C. "Okay, I can live without the nomination being unanimous."
   D. "If I get the majority of delegates' votes, I am *the* nominee!"

2. In 1948, what member of Congress, in a blistering attack at the Republican National Convention, called HST "a man of phlegm, not of fire."
   A. Joseph Martin, Massachusetts
   B. Claire Boothe Luce, Connecticut
   C. Martin Dies, Texas
   D. Everett Dirksen, Illinois

3. Who did *not* run against HST in the 1948 presidential election?
   A. Henry A Wallace, former vice president
   B. Strom Thurman, governor of South Carolina
   C. Thomas Dewey, governor of New York
   D. Robert Taft, senator, Ohio

4. Where did HST predict, "Senator Barkley and I will win this election and make these Republicans like it—don't you forget that!"
   A. During his acceptance speech at the Democratic National Convention in Philadelphia
   B. At a press conference when he announced Barkley was his choice for vice president
   C. Repeatedly on the whistle-stop campaign
   D. At his first White House press conference after accepting the nomination in Philadelphia

5. Why did "Dixiecrats," headed by Governor Strom Thurman, oppose HST's reelection in 1948?

A. HST's advocacy of civil rights
B. HST's "desegregation" of the military
C. HST's insistence that all black veterans have full citizenship including the right to run for public office
D. HST providing full veterans' benefits to black veterans

6. What did HST call the 80th Congress that he, during the campaign of 1948, called back into session?
   A. "The snail-Congress"
   B. "The no-good, do-nothing Congress"
   C. "The lazy-as-hell Congress"
   D. "The slowpoke Congress"

7. What newspaper editorialized that HST lacked "the stature, the vision, the social, and economic grasp, or the sense of history required to lead the nation in a world crisis"?
   A. *The St. Louis Post-Dispatch*
   B. *The New York Times*
   C. *The Los Angeles Times*
   D. *The Wall Street Journal*

8. In 1948, what did many angry housewives call HST?
   A. "A *Demon*crat"
   B. "Horsemeat Harry"
   C. "That mousy little haberdasher"
   D. "The little man with a full stomach!"

9. Who said of HST "One day I find in him a dedicated public servant and the next time I find him to be a Pendergast-machine politician who will do anything for a vote."?
   A. Herbert Hoover
   B. J. Edgar Hoover
   C. Yogi Berra
   D. Henry Cabot Lodge

10. At a campaign stop in Waco, Texas, why did the crowd boo HST?

    A. He talked about the University of Texas being in Waco
    B. He shook hands with a black woman
    C. He pointed out that the name Dewey rhymes with hooey
    D. He declared, "It's past time that Texans realize that when the Constitution says all it meant *all!*"

11. In a campaign speech in the Mormon Tabernacle in Salt Lake City, Harry talked about what?

    A. His deep commitment to religious liberty for all
    B. His grandfather's trading trips to the city
    C. His strong opposition to infidelity and divorce
    D. The importance of separation of church and state

12. What did HST demand before speaking at Rebel Stadium in Dallas in 1948?

    A. That no one would try to put a cowboy hat on him
    B. That seating be integrated
    C. That collection buckets be passed
    D. That no rebel flags be displayed

13. What did HST say the GOP stood for?

    A. Gluttons of Privilege
    B. Gladiators of the Past
    C. Generators of Pessimism
    D. Gobblers of Phoniness

14. In October 1948, in St. Paul, Minnesota, campaigning for Hubert Humphrey running for the Senate, what did HST say about the Republicans' stance on health care?

    A. "Any government aid to health care will lead to socialism."
    B. "They say, 'Trust the AMA. Trust the AMA'"

C. "They think modern medical care and hospitals are just fine—for people who can afford them."

D. "Doctor knows best."

15. After the 1948 election, HST often invited people he met to visit him in Key West. Who took him up on his invitation?

A. Two sleeping-car porters
B. A railroad policeman
C. A railroad maintenance engineer
D. Two White House messengers

16. What problem on the second whistle-stop train plagued HST?

A. Fresh laundry
B. "Godawful food"
C. Sometimes there were no funds to get the train to the next stop
D. "Every Tom, Dick, and Harry Democratic politician wants to be seen riding the train—but not beside me."

17. In 1948, flying home to Independence, HST waited until the plane was over Ohio, the home of Republican Senator Robert Taft, to do what?

A. Take a nap
B. Endorse Taft's opponent
C. Use the toilet
D. Gather reporters on board to denounce "Senator Head-in-the-Sand Taft."

18. In 1948, of what group of voters did Truman declare: "If they don't do their duty by the Democratic party, they are the most ungrateful people in the world"?

A. Union members
B. Older adults
C. Military
D. Farmers

19. HST sat at the controls of a locomotive heading to Columbus, Ohio, at 65 mph. How did the president respond when an engineer asked if he had any "mechanical ability"?

    A. "I haven't had this much fun since I've been president."
    B. "One thing for damn sure: FDR as president never got to do this."
    C. "I guess a man who can hold the throttle on the U.S. government ought to be able to master a diesel locomotive for a short while."
    D. "Dewey would be too afraid of getting his clothes dirty to do this!"

20. What was something HST regularly did that surprised employees on the campaign train?

    A. Washed his own socks and underwear
    B. Generously tipped
    C. Always asked questions about their families
    D. Never ate dessert

21. When HST said, "I like Old Joe" [Stalin]..." but he's "a prisoner of the Politburo," critics pounced. What did the president admit to his press secretary?

    A. "Well, I guess I goofed."
    B. "Hell, tell me I didn't say that!"
    C. "Okay, at the next stop I'll say he's a short, rotten son of a bitch."
    D. "Get me some bourbon so I can think."

22. At a stop in San Bernardino, California, what did HST say after being presented a basket of eggs?

    A. "Some of those Republicans would have wanted them fried sunny-side down with a side of bacon and two slices of buttered bread."
    B. "At least they didn't throw them at me."
    C. "The Boss can use these for breakfast."
    D. "Were these laid by a Democratic hen?"

23. When Truman told farmers that he could "plow a furrow behind a pair of mules as straight as the next man," whom did he suggest they ask for verification?

    A. His sister
    B. His mother
    C. "Preacher Bowman at the Baptist Church in Grandview"
    D. "A blind man who lives on a farm near us"

24. In Iowa, HST told farmers that "the most peaceful thing in the world is riding behind a mule plowing a field." Why did he think that?

    A. "Mules never get in a hurry."
    B. "Mules have enough sense to know when it is time to quit for the day."
    C. "Tractors make a noise that interferes with a man's thoughts."
    D. "Mules never think they are a racehorse."

25. Why did Margaret Truman say her father didn't mind getting up at 5:00 a.m.?"

    A. "That gives him a couple extra hours to work."
    B. "The early bird gets the worm… and reelected."
    C. "He thinks that's when every right-thinking American gets up."
    D. "It gives him more time to give Republicans hell."

26. At a stop in Uvalde, Texas, what did HST give former vice president, John Nance Gardner "to use in case of snakebite."

    A. A jackknife with a presidential seal
    B. A tube of Missouri Muleskinner salve
    C. A tourniquet with a vice presidential seal on it
    D. The same expensive Kentucky bourbon that John Nance Garner had served while Truman was in the Senate.

27. What happened to all the cakes delivered to HST's train on his 66th birthday?
   A. The cakes were eaten by reporters and staff on the train.
   B. The cakes were taken off the train and send anonymously to nearby hospitals.
   C. The cakes were passed on to local Democratic campaign staff.
   D. After a few ceremonial slices were sampled, the cakes were sent to local schools.

28. At a campaign stop in Spokane, Washington, HST visited a livestock show. What did he say after a large blue ribbon was pinned on his suit?
   A. "Some Republicans will say that I stole this..."
   B. "Am I the grand champion pig or cow?"
   C. "This is the first time I've won a blue ribbon for a campaign speech."
   D. "That little man with the moustache will expect one of these if he comes through here."

29. Why were the towns where HST gave short speeches called "whistle stops"?
   A. A train engineer would toot the whistle to announce its arrival.
   B. In the time it took to whistle you missed the town
   C. Spectators were given whistles to blow when the president made a good point
   D. The president boasted that when the train stopped, he could whistle and attract a bigger crowd than his opponent.

30. Where did HST make his final 1948 campaign speech on radio?
   A. RLDS Auditorium, Independence
   B. Living room, 219 N. Delaware
   C. Large rally in the Music Hall, Kansas City
   D. The Square in front of the Jackson County Courthouse

31. How did HST mock individuals who believed the polls in 1948?
   A. "The only 'polls' that count are those in polling places in voting booths on election day!"
   B. "I wonder how far Moses would have gone if he'd taken a poll in Egypt?"
   C. "Polls cannot capture the thinking of the ordinary American."
   D. "Perhaps the good Dr. Gallup should have stayed in the classroom instead of traveling here and there predicting this and that."

32. What state did not permit Harry Truman's name on the ballot?
   A. Mississippi
   B. South Carolina
   C. Louisiana
   D. Alabama

33. What actor and future politician enthusiastically campaigned for Harry Truman in 1948?
   A. Gary Cooper
   B. Walter Pidgeon
   C. Hoagy Carmichael
   D. Ronald Reagan

34. Late in the 1948 presidential campaign, *Newsweek* polled 50 top political writers for their predictions for the winner. Not one reporter answered Truman. What did HST say when he read the article?
   A. "There isn't one of them has enough sense to pound sand in a rat hole."
   B. "Tell 'em to stick around for the finish line."
   C. "Not one of them has talked to an all-American citizen in years."
   D. "Was this poll taken before or after the bar opened?"

35. What did HST do as the results were tabulated on election night?
    A. Played high-stakes poker with friends in Independence
    B. Went for a drive to his birthplace in Lamar
    C. Had a Turkish bath, ate a ham sandwich, drank some buttermilk, and went to bed
    D. Played requests on the piano in his living room

36. *The Washington Post*, the morning after the election, unfurled a large flag on the front of their building saying what?
    A. "Mr. President, we knew you would pull it out!"
    B. "We were with you all the way!"
    C. "Mr. President, we are ready to eat crow whenever you are ready to serve it."
    D. "Give 'em more hell, Harry!"

37. HST's victory shocked the Republican establishment. Robert A. Taft, head of the conservative wing, snarled the morning after the election:
    A. "It defies all common sense to send that roughneck ward politician back to the White House."
    B. "Had we run anybody except Dewey, Harry Truman would be hightailing it back to Independence."
    C. "'The best man' did not win last night!"
    D. "God help us! The haberdasher for four more years."

38. After arriving in Key West to vacation following the grueling campaign, what did HST write his sister?
    A. "Someday we'll devise a wiser way to elect a president."
    B. "I didn't know I was so tired until I sat down."
    C. "I could not have done it without Bess and Margaret."
    D. "I love the weather here. It will be hell to have to go back to Washington."

39. How did HST explain turning away prominent visitors in Key West?
   A. "I don't give a damn how put out they get. I'm doing as I damn please for the next two years and to hell with them all."
   B. "I give them the bum's rush. I don't let them get anywhere near a chair or sofa."
   C. "They are crazy as hell if they think I am giving up vacation time to listen to them!"
   D. "I tell them to go see Thomas Dewey. He has plenty of time on his hands to see visitors."

40. What was one immediate development after HST won?
   A. Allegations that some costs of operating the whistle-stop train had broken federal laws
   B. "A flood of back-dated campaign contributions" were mailed to Truman
   C. Democratic politicians showing up at the Oval Office wanting their picture made with HST
   D. Individuals who had not participated in Truman's reelection campaign were now lobbying for government positions

41. What campaign strategy was most effective in HST's victory?
   A. Recognizing Israel
   B. Traveling 31,000 miles by train
   C. Blasting the "do-nothing" 80th Congress
   D. Selecting Alben Barkley as his running mate

42. What significantly critical act enabled HST's win?
   A. Recognizing Israel stimulated heavy Jewish vote for Truman in New York City
   B. An overconfident Republican Thomas Dewey began selecting his cabinet
   C. Truman seemed far more "human" than Dewey.
   D. The undecideds—about 15 percent—swung to Truman "very late" in the campaign.

43. What was an innovation for the 1949 inaugural?
    A. Blacks were invited to all the main inaugural events.
    B. The newest justice of the Supreme Court administered the oath of office.
    C. It was the first presidential inauguration to be televised.
    D. A president-elect's daughter held the Bible for the oath of office

44. When did HST decide that he would not run for a third term in 1952?
    A. January 24, 1949
    B. April 16, 1950
    C. November 19, 1951
    D. January 20, 1952

Election of 1948—*Answers*

1. A. "Any shithead behind this desk can get renominated." (Beschloss, 2007, p. 213)
2. B. Claire Boothe Luce, Connecticut (Morris, 2014, p. 213)
3. D. Robert Taft, senator, Ohio (Parmet, 1989, p. 116)
4. A. During his acceptance speech at the Democratic National Convention in Philadelphia (McCullough, 1992, p. 642)
5. A. HST's advocacy of civil rights (Parmet, 1989, p. 115)
6. B. "The no-good, do-nothing Congress" (Hedley, 1979, p. 174)
7. A. *The St. Louis Post-Dispatch* (Uebelhor, 2006, p. 593)
8. B. "Horsemeat Harry" (Schweikart & Lynch, 1994, p. 91)
9. A. Herbert Hoover (Jeansonne, 2016, p. 358)
10. B. He shook hands with a black woman (Ferrell, 1983, p. 103)
11. B. His grandfather's trading trips to the city (Truman, September 21, 1948)
12. B. That seating be integrated (Ferrell, 1983, pp. 102–103)
13. A. Gluttons of Privilege (Truman, 1966, 1952–1953, p. 694)
14. C. "They think modern medical care and hospitals are fine—for people who can afford them." (Truman, 1948, p. 771)
15. A. Two sleeping-car porters (Knutson, 2014, p. 264)
    B. A railroad policeman (Knutson, 2014, p. 264)
    C. A railroad maintenance engineer (Knutson, 2014, p. 264)
    D. Two White House messengers (Knutson, 2014, p. 264)
16. C. Sometimes there were no funds to get the train to the next stop (Ferrell, 1983, p. 102)

17. C. Use the toilet (Ferrell, 1983, p. 100)
18. D. Farmers (Hedley, 1979, p. 182)
19. C. "I guess a man who can hold the throttle on the U.S. government ought to be able to master a diesel locomotive for a short while." (Withers, 1996, p. 186)
20. A. Washed his own socks and underwear (Withers, 1996, p. 188)
21. A. "Well, I guess I goofed." (Withers, 1996, p. 196)
22. B. "At least they didn't throw them at me." (Withers, 1996, p. 197)
23. B. His mother (Withers, 1996, p. 201)
24. C. "Tractors make a noise that interferes with a man's thoughts." (Withers, 1996, p. 201)
25. C. "He thinks that's when every right-thinking American gets up." (Withers, 1996, p. 208)
26. D. The same expensive Kentucky bourbon that John Nance Garner had served while Truman was in the Senate. (Withers, 1996, p. 208–209)
27. B. The cakes were taken off the train and sent anonymously to nearby hospitals. (Withers, 1996, p. 230)
28. B. "Am I the grand champion pig or cow?" (Withers, 1996, p. 235)
29. A. A train engineer would toot the whistle to announce its arrival. (Hedley, 1979, p. 178)
30. B. Living room, 219 N. Delaware (Hedley, 1979, p. 184)
31. B. "I wonder how far Moses would have gone if he'd taken a poll in Egypt?" (Lepore, 2018, p. 542)
32. D. Alabama (White, 2014, p. 195)
33. D. Ronald Reagan (Peretti, 2012, pp. 92–93, 187)
34. A. "There isn't one of them has enough sense to pound sand in a rat hole." (McCullough, 1992, p. 695)
35. C. Had a Turkish bath, ate a ham sandwich, drank some buttermilk, and went to bed (Whitman, December 27, 1972, p. 46)

36. C. "Mr. President, we are ready to eat crow whenever you are ready to serve it." (Hedley, 1979, p. 186)

37. A. "It defies all common sense to send that roughneck ward politician back to the White House." (Reid, 2016, p. 347)

38. B. "I didn't know I was so tired until I sat down." (Truman, 1973, p. 394)

39. A. "I don't give a damn how put out they get. I'm doing as I damn please for the next two years and to hell with them all." (Walsh, 2005, p. 120)

40. B. "A flood of back-dated campaign contributions" were mailed to Truman (Hedley, 1979, p. 186)

41. B. Traveling 31,000 miles by train (White, 2014, p. 8)

42. D. The undecideds—about 15 percent—chose Truman "very late" in the campaign. (Allen, 1989, p. 290)

43. A. Blacks were invited to all the main inaugural events. (Donovan, 1982, p. 21)

44. B. April 16, 1950 (Donovan, 1982, p. 171)

Turmoil in China and Korea

What was MacArthur's faux pas when he met HST on Wake Island?

1. What bold action did HST take to try to stabilize China after World War II ended?

   A. Fired the U.S. ambassador
   B. Sent General Marshall as his special envoy to negotiate with the factions
   C. Threatened to cut off all U.S. aid to China
   D. Demanded that Chiang Kai-shek step down

2. HST's policy toward Chiang's China was based on what premise?

   A. The Chinese had a right to choose their own form of government
   B. The United States was taxed trying to contain the Russian threat
   C. Chiang's Nationalist government was "a lost cause."
   D. Truman, not congressional Republicans or the China Lobby, set foreign policy

3. What event on October 1, 1949, significantly challenged HST's foreign policy and relationship with Congress?

   A. The death of General George C. Marshall
   B. Mao's proclamation of the People's Republic of China
   C. Reports of Communists in the State Department influencing events in China
   D. China and Russia signed a mutual-aid pact

4. Mao's victory over Chiang forced Truman to do what?

   A. Recognize Mao's government
   B. Rethink the defense budget
   C. Recall American missionaries from China
   D. Globalize the strategy of containment

5. Who charged that HST, George Marshall, and Dean Acheson had "permitted" the fall of China to the Communists?

   A. Henry Wallace
   B. Arthur H. Vandenberg, senator from Michigan
   C. Joseph McCarthy, senator from Wisconsin
   D. Walter Judd, congressman, Minnesota

6. Which position did George C. Marshall not fill in the Truman administrations?

   A. Secretary of Defense
   B. NATO ambassador
   C. Secretary of State
   D. Special representative to China

7. What Russian development further complicated HST's policies on China in 1949?

   A. Russian detonation of an atomic bomb
   B. Death of Josef Stalin
   C. Russian recognition of Kim Il-sung, first Communist leader of North Korea
   D. Joseph McCarthy's allegations about Communist influence within the State Department

8. What major allegation was leveled against HST after 1949?

   A. That his prejudice against Asians kept him from responding compassionately to Chinese tensions
   B. That he had "lost China"
   C. That his inept foreign policy would cause more Asian nations to go communist
   D. That he believed Mao could reform China

9. In response to China's ambitions, what actions did HST take?

   A. Deployed the U.S. Seventh Fleet to patrol the Taiwan Strait
   B. Ordered U.S. military and economic aid to the

French-fighting Communist insurgents in Indochina

C. Resisted efforts within the United Nations to expel Chiang and seat Mao's representatives

D. Directed U.S. delegation to raise the Korean issue before the Security Council

10. Where did HST learn that North Korean troops had invaded South Korea?

A. In Independence celebrating his 31st wedding anniversary

B. At Independence High School attending a band concert

C. At a picnic at his brother's farm in Grandview, Missouri

D. In the foyer of First Baptist Church, Washington, DC

11. What did HST tell Secretary of State Acheson after being informed the North Korean Army had invaded South Korea?

A. "Damn, this could be the start of World War III!"

B. "Damn those little bastards...."

C. "Dean, we've got to stop the sons of bitches no matter what."

D. "MacArthur will make them regret that choice."

12. The president returned to Washington to consult with his staff. Secretary of State Acheson and Secretary of Defense Lewis Johnson met Truman at the airport. How did Truman express his determination to meet the threat?

A. "They started this, but we will finish it!"

B. "They've waved their little red flag in front of the wrong man!"

C. "By God, I'm going to let them have it!"

D. "Apparently those little bastards have forgotten what we did to Japan!"

13. What did HST identify as his main focus in Korea?
    A. "To prevent a third world war"
    B. "To show Stalin that the United States would not ignore overlook Communist aggression anywhere on the globe!"
    C. "To fully support the United Nations"
    D. "The war was a moral fight between freedom of religion and godless communism."

14. Who did HST believe ordered the invasion of southern Korea?
    A. Josef Stalin
    B. Mao Zedong
    C. Kim Il Sung
    D. Chiang Kai-shek

15. "If we let Korea go under" what consequences did HST predict?
    A. "The Soviet[s] will keep right on going and swallow up one [place] after another."
    B. "We will have no credibility anywhere on the globe where the Communists choose to test us."
    C. "The peace of the world will unravel."
    D. "The Republicans will impeach me!"

16. In a meeting with congressional leaders, how did HST try to pacify their concerns that he had not consulted Congress before sending troops to Korea?
    A. "If there is any necessity for congressional action, I will come to you. But I hope we can get those bandits in Korea suppressed without that."
    B. "And what? Sit around waiting for you to debate while South Korea goes to hell...."
    C. "I am not about to commit myself to consulting Congress before taking drastic steps in Korea."
    D. "When I want a declaration of war, I'll let you know."

17. When Indiana Senator William Jenner insisted that Congress either seek a declaration of war or bring home every American serviceman, how did HST respond?

A. "I don't tell that old son of a bitch how to do his job so where does he get off trying to tell me how to do mine?"

B. "I don't believe Senator Jenner was a war hero."

C. "I don't ask their permission—I just consult them."

D. "That old buzzard has never read the Constitution."

18. How did HST respond when Dean Rusk, a presidential aide, suggested Chiang's Formosa might be the next Russian target?

A. "I will not give Chiang 'a nickel' for any purpose whatever."

B. "Madame Chiang Kai-shek will have to use her 'influence' on Congress to get money."

C. "The Russians could do the world a big favor and get rid of that little thief."

D. "You have to consider the Russians will try something in Eastern Europe."

19. What was HST's initial military goal of the United States in Korea?

A. To drive North Korean troops out of South Korea

B. To liberate North Korea from communism

C. To keep Russian supplies from North Korea soldiers

D. To reunify Korea

20. What did HST call the hostilities in Korea?

A. "A police action"

B. "The fuse for World War III"

C. "A lite little war"

D. "The barrier to World War III"

21. In July 1950, what were the results of Gallup's American public opinion polls on Truman's Korean policy?
    A. 80% approved of the decision to intervene
    B. 75% thought intervention could lead to world peace
    C. 95% thought Douglas MacArthur was the right leader to clean up the mess in Korea
    D. 65% believed that HST should give MacArthur carte blanche in Korea

22. In 1950, when an aide began describing how the war in Korea could be spun politically, how did HST respond?
    A. "If there is any political heat—I will take it!"
    B. "This is about preventing World War III. This isn't about politics or politicians!"
    C. "We're not going to talk about politics! I'll handle the political affairs!"
    D. "I am acting as commander-in-chief—not a politician!"

23. In a moment of frustration, how did HST characterize congressional critics of his Korean policies?
    A. "Liars, trimmers and pussyfooters on both sides of the aisle."
    B. "Buzzards waiting to pick the meat off my carcass."
    C. "Morons who have no idea how tough it is to deal with the Chinese, the Russians, and His Excellency MacArthur all at the same time."
    D. "The main thing those birds think about is their next election campaign."

24. Who, challenging Truman's war strategy in a letter to Congress, declared, "There is no substitute for victory!"
    A. Governor Thomas Dewey

B. General Douglas MacArthur

C. President Syngman Rhee of South Korea

D. Senator Strom Thurmond

25. What did HST call General Douglas MacArthur?

A. "The stupidest man wearing an American uniform."

B. "One arrogant son of a bitch."

C. "Mr. Prima Donna, Brass Hat, Five Star MacArthur."

D. "A first-class warmonger—pure and simple."

26. En route to meet General MacArthur in Wake Island, HST stopped in California and visited wounded Korean soldiers with what well-known entertainer?

A. Bob Hope

B. Olivia de Haviland

C. Ronald Reagan

D. Harpo Marx

27. What prominent Republican urged HST to recall General MacArthur?

A. John Foster Dulles

B. Thomas Dewey

C. Everett Dirksen

D. Margaret Chase Smith

28. In a letter written while flying to Wake Island, how did HST describe his anxiety about meeting MacArthur?

A. "I was not this apprehensive meeting Churchill or Stalin."

B. "I've a whale of a job before me. Have to talk to God's right-hand man."

C. "I hope I am not walking into a political ambush."

D. "Well, if Abe Lincoln could go meet General McClellan, I guess it was alright for me to come out here to meet MacArthur."

29. When HST questioned MacArthur about the chances of the Chinese intervening in Korea, how did the general answer?
    A. The Chinese would not dare come in.
    B. If they intervene, MacArthur's forces will destroy them.
    C. He did not think much of the strength of Mao's forces.
    D. The police action will be over by Thanksgiving, i.e., in six weeks.

30. What was MacArthur's faux pas when he met HST on Wake Island?
    A. His shirt was unbuttoned.
    B. He wore a greasy "ham-and-eggs" cap.
    C. He failed to salute the commander-in-chief.
    D. He kept Truman waiting 15 minutes.

31. How did HST respond to a call from General Omar Bradley informing him that more than a quarter million Chinese troops were now in North Korea?
    A. "Oh, my God! Are you sure there wasn't a mistake in deciphering the cable?"
    B. "Those stupid sons of bitches!"
    C. "This is the worst situation we have had yet. We'll just have to meet it like all the rest."
    D. "I bet ole MacArthur wet himself when he heard this!"

32. During the Korean War, HST asked for contingency plans for what radical idea?
    A. To destroy Soviet air bases in the Far East
    B. To arrange a secret meeting with Chairman Mao
    C. To transfer a dozen atomic bombs to South Korea
    D. To order extensive food and gasoline rationing

33. How did HST brand the forces attacking South Korea?
    A. "Cannon-fodder!"

B. "Impoverished serfs in military uniforms"

C. "A bunch of bandits"

D. "Individuals brainwashed by Communist propaganda"

34. On November 30, 1950, HST created a stir in a press conference, by saying, "We will take whatever steps are necessary to meet the military situation." A reporter then asked, "Will that include the atomic bomb?" How did HST answer?

A. "Use of the atomic bomb is on the table as we speak."

B. "That includes every weapon we have."

C. "The bomb ended the war in Japan. It could end this war and save thousands of American lives."

D. "The reason you develop weapons is to use them!"

35. What prompted HST to "recall" or fire General Douglas MacArthur, the commander of United Nations forces defending South Korea on April 11, 1951?

A. MacArthur's growing interest in running for president in 1952

B. MacArthur's strategy to bomb the North Korea/China border

C. MacArthur "backchanneling" Republicans to gain support for his war strategy

D. MacArthur's pressuring Truman for permission to use atomic bombs

36. Following a leak of the decision to recall MacArthur, what did the president say?

A. "Now I will have to kiss his ass on the White House lawn."

B. "That man has friends everywhere...."

C. "That demagogue will try to spin this into an attack on the military."

D. "That son of a bitch isn't going to resign on me—I want him fired!"

37. After returning to the United States, MacArthur addressed a joint session of Congress. How did HST assess that speech?
   A. "Disgusting!"
   B. "Bullshit! Plain unadulterated bullshit."
   C. "Damn fool Congressmen [were] crying like a bunch of women" after hearing "nothing but a bunch of bullshit."
   D. "MacArthur thinks he's the reincarnation of the ancient orator Demosthenes."

38. By late fall 1951, what percentage of Americans approved of Truman's handling of the Korean War?
   A. 23%
   B. 38%
   C. 50.6%
   D. 83%

39. What Republican senator denounced HST's "limited war" in Korea as "appeasement" and declared that he should consider dropping the atomic bomb on "those barbarians"—the Chinese Communists?
   A. Robert A. Taft, Ohio
   B. Margaret Chase Smith, Maine
   C. Kenneth Wherry, Nebraska
   D. Joseph McCarthy, Wisconsin

40. What was "the most trying" element for HST during this conflict?
   A. Being unable to disclose all the details that contributed to his military strategy.
   B. Dealing with the "prima donna" MacArthur.
   C. Awarding the Medal of Honor to heroes or their survivors.
   D. Writing condolence letters to families of casualties.

41. How did HST's assess Republican presidential candidate Eisenhower's promise, "I will go to Korea"?

A. "One half-assed idea!"
B. "Just a piece of demagoguery"
C. "The General's Folly!"
D. "Now Ike wants to be the prima donna!"

42. Dwight Eisenhower, HST's successor, agreed to an armistice signed on July 27, 1953. What did this agreement *not* provide?
    A. POWs had to return to their country of origin.
    B. North Korea took control of an extra 1,500 square miles of territory near the 38th parallel.
    C. Both sides agreed to a two-mile-wide "demilitarized zone."
    D. Both sides would hold a referendum on reuniting the country within one year.

43. Of the nearly four million civilian and military deaths, how many Americans died?
    A. Approximately 24,012
    B. Approximately 31,475
    C. Approximately 33,629
    D. Approximately 62,274

44. What did the Korean War demonstrate on the issue of civil rights?
    A. That all blood flows red
    B. That non-segregated units functioned better with white leaders
    C. That blacks needed opportunities for promotion
    D. That a non-segregated army was more efficient than a segregated one

Turmoil in China and Korea—*Answers*

1. B. Sent General Marshall as his special envoy to negotiate with the factions (Doenecke, 1989, p. 48)
2. C. Chiang's Nationalist government was "a lost cause." (Brands, 2010, p. 49)
3. B. Mao's proclamation of the People's Republic of China (Peraino, 2017, pp. 211–212)
4. D. Globalize the strategy of containment (Peraino, 2017, p. 264)
5. C. Joseph McCarthy, senator from Wisconsin (Marshall, 2006, p. 387)
6. B. NATO ambassador (Marshall, 2006, p. 387)
7. A. Russian detonation of an atomic bomb (Leffler, 1992, p. 327)
   B. Death of Josef Stalin (Leffler, 1992, p. 327)
   C. Russian recognition of Kim Il-sung, first Communist leader of North Korea (Leffler, 1992, p. 327)
   D. Joseph McCarthy's allegations of Communist influence within the State Department (Leffler, 1992, p. 327)
8. B. That he had "lost China" (Brands, 2010, p. 49)
9. A. Deployed the U.S. Seventh Fleet to patrol the Taiwan Strait (Brands, 2010, p. 56)
   B. Ordered U.S. military and economic aid to the French-fighting Communist insurgents in Indochina (Brands, 2010, p. 56)
   C. Resisted efforts within the United Nations to expel Chiang and seat Mao's representatives (Brands, 2010, p. 56)
   D. Directed U.S. delegation to raise the Korean issue before the Security Council (Brands, 2010, p. 56)
10. A. In Independence celebrating his 31st wedding anniversary (Hamby, 1995, p. 533)

11. C. "Dean, we've got to stop the sons of bitches no matter what." (Hamby, 1995, p. 534)

12. C. "By God, I'm going to let them have it!" (Ferrell, 1983, p. 116)

13. A. "To prevent a third world war" (Donovan, 1982, p. 359)

14. A. Josef Stalin (Leffler, 1992, p. 367; Hamby, 1995, p. 536)

15. A. "The Soviet[s] will keep right on going and swallow up one [place] after another." (Truman, January 15, 1953)

16. A. "If there is any necessity for congressional action, I will come to you. But I hope we can get those bandits in Korea suppressed without that." (Beschloss, 2018, p. 457)

17. C. "I don't ask their permission—I just consult them." (Beschloss, 2018, p. 472)

18. A. "I will not give Chiang 'a nickel' for any purpose whatever." (Beschloss, 2018, p. 450)

19. A. To drive North Korean troops out of South Korea (Brands, 2010, p. 57)

20. A. "A police action" (Hamby, 1995, p. 537)

21. A. 80% approved of the decision to intervene (Rose, 1999, p. 192)

22. C. "We're not going to talk about politics! I'll handle the political affairs!" (Beschloss, 2018, p. 447)

23. A. "Liars, trimmers and pussyfooters on both sides of the aisle." (Beschloss, 2018, p. 472)

24. B. General Douglas MacArthur (McCullough, 1992, p. 838)

25. C. "Mr. Prima Donna, Brass Hat, Five Star MacArthur" (Leonard, 2006, p. 347)

26. D. Harpo Marx (Beschloss, 2018, p. 465)

27. A. John Foster Dulles (Beschloss, 2018, p. 455)

28. B. "I've a whale of a job before me. Have to talk to God's right-hand man" (Sides, 2018, p. 58)

29. D. The police action will be over by Thanksgiving, i.e., in six weeks. (Sides, 2018, p. 59)

30. A. His shirt was unbuttoned. (Sides, 2018, p. 58)

   B. He wore a greasy "ham-and-eggs" cap. (Sides, 2018, p. 58)

   C. He failed to salute the commander-in-chief. (Sides, 2018, p. 58)

31. C. "This is the worst situation we have had yet. We'll just have to meet it like all the rest." (Sides, 2018, p. 196)

32. A. To destroy Soviet air bases in the Far East (Beschloss, 2018, p. 446)

33. C. "A bunch of bandits" (Beschloss, 2018, p. 453)

34. B. "That includes every weapon we have." (Sides, 2018, p. 238)

35. C. MacArthur "backchanneling" Republicans to gain support for his war strategy (McCullough, 1992, p. 838)

36. D. "That son of a bitch isn't going to resign on me—I want him fired!" (Beschloss, 2018, p. 446)

37. C. "Damn fool Congressmen [were] crying like a bunch of women" after hearing "nothing but a bunch of bullshit." (Beschloss, 2018, p. 475)

38. A. 23% (Pemberton, 1989, p. 157)

39. B. Margaret Chase Smith, Maine (Tracy, 2006, p. 531)

40. C. Awarding the Medal of Honor to heroes or their survivors (Truman, 1973, p. 525)

41. B. "Just a piece of demagoguery" (Beschloss, 2018, p. 486)

42. A. POWs had to return to their country of origin. (McCullough, 1992, p. 935)

43. C. Approximately 33,629 (McCullough, 1992, p. 935)
44. D. That a non-segregated army was more efficient than a segregated one (Truman, 1956, p. 183)

Civil Rights

*How did Tom Connally of Texas,
with whom HST had served in the
Senate, dismiss the president's
proposals on civil rights?*

1. Aboard the Roosevelt funeral train, how did Senator Burnet Maybank, D-South Carolina, reassure one colleague about the new president's attitudes on race?
   A. "Everything's going to be all right—the new president knows how to handle the niggers."
   B. "He won't let Mrs. [Bess] Truman go around stirring up the negroes like Eleanor did."
   C. "Just remember this: Truman is from Missouri."
   D. "Truman won't be able to pass anything without southern votes."

2. What racial incident in the South in 1946 sickened HST and prompted him to bellow, "Enough is enough!"
   A. A lynching in Louisiana
   B. The blinding of a black soldier Isaac Woodard
   C. The murders of four young African Americans: George and Mae Murray Dorsey, and Roger and Dorothy Malcomb by a white mob
   D. Race riots in Columbia, Tennessee, that turned violent

3. What did HST do when he learned that a Sioux City, Iowa, cemetery had stopped the committal service of John R. Rice, a soldier killed in Korea, because he was "not Caucasian"?
   A. Arranged to have Sgt. Rice buried in Arlington
   B. Asked the Iowa governor to review the tax status of the cemetery
   C. Demanded that both Iowa senators intervene
   D. Signed an executive order that no veteran could be buried in that cemetery until its discriminatory regulations be repealed

4. When four black citizens were killed near the home of a southern segregationist senator, Richard Russell of Georgia, how did HST react?
   A. "Russell has always been a Klanner—this shouldn't be a surprise!"
   B. "My God, I had no idea it was as terrible as that. We've got to do something."
   C. "I need to lubricate the senator's memory with a little bourbon."
   D "Hell, I'm surprised it didn't happen in his barn!"

5. Advised that 1948 was "not the year" to push civil rights, how did HST respond?
   A. "There has *never* been a better time than 1948!"
   B. "It is not about 'pushing civil rights,' it is about giving Americans their constitutional rights."
   C. "I am going to try to remedy it and if that ends up in my failure to be reelected, that failure will be in a good cause."
   D. "The president is supposed to do the right thing— not the convenient thing."

6. HST believed that all Americans were "created equal." That conclusion came from what source?
   A. The Declaration of Independence
   B. The Constitution
   C. The Bill of Rights
   D. The heroic service of African Americans in two world wars

7. What southern Democrat declined election as U.S. Senate Democratic majority leader to avoid having to advance Truman's legislative agenda?
   A. Willis Robertson of Virginia
   B. James Eastland of Mississippi
   C. Lister Hill of Alabama
   D. Richard Russell of Georgia

8. According to a Gallup Poll in 1948, what percentage of the American public, supported federal civil rights legislation?

   A. 3%
   B. 6%
   C. 18%
   D. 27%

9. How did Tom Connally of Texas, with whom HST had served in the Senate, dismiss the president's proposals on civil rights?

   A. "A lynching of the Constitution"
   B. "A full-scale assault on southern rights"
   C. "He needs to cut back on his bourbon."
   D. "The kiss of death for his reelection in '48"

10. What did HST tell the 15 distinguished Americans serving on the President's Committee on Civil Rights?

    A. "I want to find out just how far we can go."
    B. "I want a report from you that will stir up some hell!"
    C. "Do not pay any attention to what Richard Russell's gang in the Senate will say!"
    D. "You have an opportunity to make the Constitution apply to every American! And I mean every one!"

11. What was a significant "first" on HST's whistle-stop trains?

    A. The inclusion of black reporters
    B. Television coverage
    C. Use of primitive computers
    D. An onboard rolling laundry

12. Peeved, HST, on the floor of the 1948 Democratic National Convention, told a reporter from the prominent black newspaper, the *Pittsburgh Courier*, what?

    A. "Harry Truman has never been a racist and he won't change to win this election!"
    B. "I have always been for equality of opportunity in work, working conditions, and political rights."
    C. "Here's a headline for your front page, 'Truman says civil rights for *all*! A-L-L!'"
    D. "I am president of the United States—and will not be thwarted by a bunch of people with a warped understanding of the Constitution! By God, *all* means all!"

13. A reporter at the 1948 Democratic National Convention asked Strom Thurman, the segregationist governor of South Carolina, to comment on HST's commitment to civil rights. Wasn't Truman only saying the same empty things that FDR had said? How did the senator answer?

    A. "I agree. But he [Truman] really means it."
    B. "Perhaps. But Truman's stubborn as a mule. When he takes a stance he won't back down."
    C. "People get tired of an ole dog barking."
    D. "Well, Mr. Truman had better stay the hell out of Dixie!"

14. At the 1948 Democratic National Convention, Senator Richard Russell was nominated as a challenge to HST by a young Alabama legislator named George Wallace who bitterly opposed HST's policies. What did Wallace contend in nominating Russell to deny HST the nomination?

    A. That "Democrats would have a clear choice not to go to hell with a Pied-Piper named Truman!"
    B. "Senator Russell will be Thomas Dewey's and Harry Truman's worst nightmare."

C. "Senator Russell will make sure that the South is "not crucified on the cross of the so-called civil rights program."
D. "This is the last chance to stop Truman from betraying the South."

15. How did Mississippi's largest newspaper, *The Jackson Daily News*, editorialize opposition to HST in 1948?
A. "Truman might be elected president of the United States but *not of the sovereign state of Mississippi!*"
B. "Dewey offers Mississippi voters a chance not to follow a Pied-Piper named Truman into the quagmire of miscegenation!"
C. "Mississippi has as much use for Truman as a bull has for a brassiere."
D. "If Truman should somehow carry Mississippi, our electors in the electoral college will not cast their votes for him."

16. Believing actions spoke louder than words, what action in 1949 did he take that demonstrated his commitment to equal opportunity before the law?
A. Chose a black pastor to pray at the inauguration
B. Hosted black guests overnight in the White House
C. Opened all the events of the inauguration to blacks
D. Appointed William H. Hastie to the Third Circuit Court of Appeals—the first African American to serve on the federal bench.

17. What Truman observation in *The New York Times* in 1960 prompted Martin Luther King, Jr. to demand an apology?
A. "Negro leaders today tend to forget how much they got from my administration."
B. "The southern lunch counter demonstrations have been engineered by Communists."
C. "Rev. King needs to stick to preaching."
D. "Rev. King needs to stay home and care for his flock."

18. How did HST characterize the activist Freedom Riders?
    A. "Northern busybodies"
    B. "Bad citizens"
    C. "Meddlesome intruders"
    D. "Dopey Russian pawns"

Civil Rights—*Answers*

1. A. "Everything's going to be all right—the new president knows how to handle the niggers." (Leuchtenburg, 2005, p. 162)
2. B. The blinding of a black soldier Isaac Woodard (Gergel, 2019, p.137)
3. A. Arranged to have Sgt. Rice buried in Arlington (McCullough, 1992, p. 860)
4. B. "My God, I had no idea it was as terrible as that. We've got to do something." (Burnes, 2003, p. 173)
5. C. "I am going to try to remedy it and if that ends up in my failure to be reelected, that failure will be in a good cause." (Ferrell, 1983, p. 98)
6. A. The Declaration of Independence (Truman, June 28, 1947)
   B. The Constitution
   C. The Bill of Rights
7. D. Richard Russell of Georgia (*The New York Times*, 2018, p. A15)
8. B. 6% (White, 2014, p. 82)
9. A. "A lynching of the Constitution" (McCullough, 1992, p. 588)
10. A. "I want to find out just how far we can go." (Leuchtenburg, 2005, p. 167)
11. A. The inclusion of black reporters (White, 2014, p. 222)
12. B. "I have always been for equality of opportunity in work, working conditions, and political rights." (Geselbracht, 2007, p. 190)
13. A. "I agree. But he [Truman] really means it." (Truman, 1956, p. 183)
14. C. "Senator Russell will make sure that the South is "not crucified on the cross of the so-called civil rights program." (Leuchtenburg, 2005, p. 193)

15. C. "Mississippi has as much use for Truman as a bull has for a brassiere." (Leuchtenburg, 2005, p. 181)

16. D. Appointed William H. Hastie to the Third Circuit Court of Appeals—the first African American to serve on the federal bench. (Gardiner, 2002, p. 33)

17. B. "The southern lunch counter demonstrations have been engineered by Communists." (Truman is asked to prove charge, April 20, 1960)

18. A. "Northern busybodies." (Giglio, 1989, p. 305)

   B. "Bad citizens" (Giglio, 1989, p. 305)

McCarthyism

HST believed that Senators Mc-Carthy, Wherry, and Bridges were attempting to sabotage the foreign policy of the United States. How did he underscore his opinion?

1. How did Senator Joseph McCarthy react to HST's sacking of General Douglas MacArthur?

   A. "The son of a bitch ought to be impeached after making a decision while drunk on bourbon and Benedictine."

   B. "That son of a bitch ought to be thoroughly and swiftly impeached."

   C. "Truman's Stalin's most effective stooge."

   D. "Truman's not good enough to polish MacArthur's boots!"

2. Who was McCarthy's most useful ally?

   A. Martin Dies, chair of House Special Committee to Investigate Un-American Activities

   B. J. Edgar Hoover, director of the FBI

   C. William Randolph Hearst, newspaper owner and publisher

   D. John L. Lewis, labor leader

3. HST commented, "In a free country we punish men for the crimes they commit but never for the opinions they have," in responding to what?

   A. McCarthy's inflammatory speech to a Republican women's club in West Virginia

   B. Congress's passage of the McCarran Internal Security Act

   C. Reports of FBI investigations into private lives of politicians

   D. Allegations against the distinguished scientist, Edward U. Condon.

4. What did HST say about McCarthyism in a speech to the American Legion's annual convention in 1952?

   A. "McCarthy and his ilk are a far bigger threat to America than Joe Stalin and his cronies in Moscow."

154

B. McCarthy and his slandermongers "are trying to get us so hysterical that no one will stand up to them" and risk "being called a Communist."

C. "'Freedom of speech' does not cover McCarthy's reckless blabber."

D. "Maybe it's time to take a closer look at 'Tailgunner Joe's' heroic war record!"

5. What did HST think about Senator Margaret Chase Smith's denunciation of Joseph McCarthy in June 1950?

A. Requested America's largest newspapers to run Senator Smith's remarks on their editorial pages

B. Commented: "Senator Smith is the only Republican with enough fortitude to speak out against that demagogue."

C. Invited her to dinner at the White House

D. Praised her words as "one of the finest things that has happened here in Washington in my years in the Senate and White House."

6. HST believed that Senators McCarthy, Wherry, and Bridges were attempting to sabotage the foreign policy of the United States. How did he underscore his opinion?

A. This "is just as bad in this cold war as it would be to shoot our soldiers in the back in a hot war."

B. "This is the worst example in American history of politicians trying to tie the president's hands on foreign policy."

C. "They should carefully read the Constitution: The president and the executive branch have the largest responsibility for foreign policy."

D. "I am hoping the Supreme Court will say to McCarthy and his ignorant pals: 'Butt out!'"

7. In private, how did HST characterize Senator McCarthy?
   A. "A pathological liar"
   B. "The sorriest excuse for a senator in that body's history"
   C. "The Kremlin's greatest asset"
   D. "A demagogue of the first order"

8. Even after HST left office, McCarthy periodically lambasted him. Finally, in November 1953, HST had had enough. What did he say on CBS Radio about his adversary?
   A. "McCarthy is a colossal disgrace!"
   B. "His name has taken on a dictionary definition meaning 'the corruption of truth.'"
   C. "McCarthy's allegations are about political advantage not truth."
   D. "Joseph McCarthy is a bully and a thug. He is the epitome of 'anti-Americanism' today."

9. When the House Special Committee to Investigate Un-American Activities subpoenaed the former president, how did HST respond?
   A. He refused to appear.
   B. He blistered the committee in an op-ed piece in *The New York Times*.
   C. "Let 'em come to Missouri and try to serve that subpoena!"
   D. "If McCarthy was on fire, I wouldn't walk across the street to piss on him!"

McCarthyism—*Answers*

1. A. "The son of a bitch ought to be impeached after making a decision while drunk on bourbon and Benedictine." (Donovan, 1982, p. 359)
2. B. J. Edgar Hoover, director of the FBI (Baughman, 2006, p. 354)
3. B. Congress's passage of the McCarran Internal Security Act (Truman, 1956, p. 284)
4. B. McCarthy and his slandermongers "are trying to get us so hysterical that no one will stand up to them" and risk "being called a Communist" (Hillstrom, 2011, p. 55)
5. D. Praised her words as "one of the finest things that has happened here in Washington in my years in the Senate and White House." (Wallace, 1995, p. 108)
6. A. This "is just as bad in this cold war as it would be to shoot our soldiers in the back in a hot war." (Miller, 2012, p. 299)
7. A. "A pathological liar" (Dallek, 2008, p. 103)
   C. "The Kremlin's greatest asset" (Truman, 1973, p. 429)
8. B. "His name has taken on a dictionary definition meaning 'the corruption of truth.'" (Truman, November 1953)
9. A. He refused to appear. (Hamby, 1995, p. 621)

Critics

Critics often pointed to HST's alleged membership in what organization?

1. What America military leader snarled, after learning that HST had become president, "It seems very unfortunate [that]... people are made vice president, who are never intended, neither by party nor by the Lord to be president."
   A. General Omar Bradley
   B. Admiral Chester Nimitz
   C. General George Patton
   D. General Dwight Eisenhower

2. When Henry Morgenthau, secretary of the treasury, learned that he was not accompanying HST to Potsdam and threatened to resign, what did the president say?
   A. "Henry, some knucklehead left you off the list to get you upset with me."
   B. "All right, if that is the way you feel, I'll accept your resignation right now."
   C. "Someone has to stay here to keep an eye on those birds in Congress."
   D. "Now, Henry, don't be a damn fool! I need you more than President Roosevelt ever did!"

3. What senator blasted HST's Korean policy saying, "In heaven's name let's not slaughter any more youngsters over there when it looks as if they are going to run us out of there anyway"?
   A. Kenneth Spicer Wherry of Nebraska
   B. Estes Kefauver of Tennessee
   C. Robert Taft of Ohio
   D. Everett Dirksen of Illinois

4. Who branded HST "the greatest appeaser in history"?
   A. Douglas MacArthur
   B. Richard M. Nixon
   C. Walter Winchell, syndicated columnist
   D. Walter Lippmann, journalist

5. Who vilified HST as "a malignant, scheming sort of an individual...totally unfit" to be president?
   A. John L. Lewis
   B. Thomas Dewey
   C. Strom Thurmond
   D. Patrick Anthony McCarran

6. During the 1948 Democratic National Convention, who wailed that HST "... has stabbed us in the back with his damnable program..."
   A. James Eastland
   B. Henry Wallace
   C. Strom Thurmond
   D. Frank M. Dixon

7. What loud critic of HST, chair of the House Special Committee to Investigate Un-American Activities, was convicted of padding his congressional payroll and sent to prison?
   A. John S. Wood
   B. John Rankin
   C. Karl Mundt
   D. John Parnell Thomas

8. What senator attacked HST's programs as "the Farewell Deal" nothing more than a "blueprint for socialism"?
   A. James O. Eastland
   B. Thomas Connally
   C. Forrest C. Donnell
   D. Kenneth S. Wherry

9. What Democrat working zealously to draft Eisenhower to run for the White House, was lambasted by HST in a private meeting: "Get this straight, whether you like it or not, I am going to be the next president of the United States. That will be all. Good day."

A. James Roosevelt
B. Willis Robertson
C. Henry Wallace
D. Joseph P. Kennedy

10. In a campaign speech in 1952 in Arkansas, who charged that HST, Dean Acheson, and Adlai Stevenson were "traitors of the high principles in which many of the nation's Democrats believe"?
    A. Harold E. Stassen
    B. Richard Nixon
    C. Dwight Eisenhower
    D. Roy Cohen

11. Critics often pointed to HST's alleged membership in what organization?
    A. Knights of the White Camelia
    B. National Federation for Constitutional Liberties
    C. Ku Klux Klan
    D. Washington Bookshop Association

12. Mrs. Robert Taft, whose husband was a strong critic of the president, is credited with originating what phrase?
    A. "Who the hell is Harry S Truman?"
    B. "I'm just mild about Harry."
    C. "To err is Truman."
    D. "Truman—that little man who lives in a big house at taxpayer's expense."

13. What political adversary eventually eulogized HST: "He did what had to be done, when it had to be done, and because he did the world today is a better and safer place—and generations to come will be in his debt"?
    A. Richard Nixon
    B. Strom Thurmond
    C. Thomas Dewey
    D. Emperor Hirohito

Critics—*Answers*

1. C. General George Patton (McCullough, 1992, p. 350)
2. B. "All right, if that is the way you feel, I'll accept your resignation right now." (Truman, 1973, p. 265)
3. D. Everett Dirksen of Illinois (Flanders, 2006, p. 137)
4. C. Walter Winchell, syndicated columnist (Figman, 2006, p. 649)
5. A. John L. Lewis (Harrison, 2006, p. 324)
6. C. Strom Thurmond (White, 2014, p. 85)
7. D. John Parnell Thomas (Figman, 2006, p. 576)
8. D. Kenneth S. Wherry (Elliott, 2006, p. 635)
9. A. James Roosevelt (McCullough, 1992, p. 629)
10. B. Richard Nixon (Summers, 2000, p. 498)
11. C. Ku Klux Klan (Robbins, 1979, p. 61; McCullough, 1992, pp. 159, 330)
12. C. "To err is Truman." (Robbins, 1979, p. 143; McCullough, 1992, p. 493)
13. A. Richard Nixon (Nixon, December 26, 1972)

Observations and Assessments

What did HST say was the most important decision he made during his presidency?

1. If the Russians boycotted the founding of the United Nations in San Francisco, HST suggested they could do what?
   A. "Forget any future Lend-Lease shipments."
   B. "Kiss goodbye any discussion about restructuring their debt to American taxpayers."
   C. "Go to hell!"
   D. "Kiss my ass in front of the Library of Congress."

2. By the end of 1950, how did a frustrated HST describe the makeup of the 81st Congress?
   A. "Political chameleons"
   B. "Part-timers on full-time pay"
   C. "More morons than patriots"
   D. "The head-in-the-sand club"

3. How did HST characterize Kenneth Spicer Wherry, the Republican Senate majority leader, 1949–1952?
   A. "A man who hasn't had an original thought in five decades"
   B. The "block-headed undertaker" from Nebraska
   C. "The Lord of the do-nothings!"
   D. "The only thing that man can pass is gas!"

4. What did HST call obstructionists in the State Department?
   A. "The Eastern Establishment"
   B. "The Amateurs"
   C. "The Striped-pants Boys"
   D. "The Ivy League Nincompoops"

5. How did Truman characterize FDR's sons?
   A. "Three amateurs"
   B. "Couldn't find one original idea among the three of them"
   C. "They think this country owes them a living."
   D. "Hear evil. Do evil. Think evil."

6. Where did HST say, "Two hours ago, I could have said five words and been quoted in 15 minutes in every capital of the world. Now I could talk for two hours and nobody would give a damn."
   A. Boarding the train home to Independence
   B. At a farewell luncheon at Dean Acheson's home
   C. To a reporter onboard the train headed for Independence
   D. To a bartender in the club car

7. What did HST say was the most important decision he made during his presidency?
   A. Dropping the atomic bomb
   B. Relieving General MacArthur
   C. Limiting the war to the Korean peninsula
   D. Running for election in 1948

8. HST observed "It's a recession when your neighbor loses his job." When did he think it became a depression?"
   A. "When the bureaucrats in the Treasury Department say so"
   B. "When you lose your own [job]"
   C. "When you cannot feed your children"
   D. "When Democrats say it is a depression. Republicans think every economic downturn is a depression."

9. How did HST assess the duties of the president?
   A. "The president is a glorified public relations man who spends his time flattering, kissing, and kicking people to get them to do what they are supposed to do anyway."
   B. "It's an all-day and nearly all-night job."
   C. "The president has to act for whatever is for the best of the country."
   D. "The man in the White House...represents 150 million people who can't afford a lobby[ist]."

10. How did HST characterize Richard Nixon?
    A. "Nixon is a shifty goddamn liar, and people know it."
    B. Nixon has never read the Constitution. "If he has, he doesn't understand it."
    C. "Nixon is reckless and ambitious and that is a dangerous mix."
    D. "Trickie Dickie, the opportunist"

11. Who was HST referring to when he said, "He is a dangerous man. Never has there been one like him so close to the presidency"?
    A. Barry Goldwater
    B. Richard Nixon
    C. George Wallace
    D. Sherman Adams

12. For the 1953 inauguration, what did HST say about Eisenhower's refusal to wear the traditional top hat?
    A. "That man can do any damn thing he wants to!"
    B. "Wouldn't surprise me if he shows up in his general's outfit wearing all his ribbons and medals."
    C. "I don't care if his ass hangs out."
    D. "That stupid SOB may show up in golf knickers."

13. Early in the Eisenhower administration, how did HST characterize his successor's leadership?
    A. "He is trying to remove any proof that I was ever president."
    B. "This fellow doesn't know any more about politics than a pig knows about Sunday."
    C. "He doesn't know any more about government than a hunting dog knows about Baptist doctrine."
    D. "I suspect the general has no earthly understanding what he has gotten himself into."

14. Who did HST have in mind when he predicted, "He will probably go down in history as one of the great men of our era"?

A. George C. Marshall
B. Dean Acheson
C. Winston Churchill
D. Admiral William Leahy

15. How did HST dismiss the House Special Committee to Investigate Un-American Activities?
   A. "Those misguided fellows think there's a Communist hiding in every closet and under every bed."
   B. "The most un-American activity in the whole government."
   C. "The living personification of Snow White's seven dwarfs!"
   D. "If the future of America is up to that bunch, we're done for."

16. What prompted HST to groan: "It's hell to be president"?
   A. Restrictive Secret Service requirements after the assassination attempt
   B. Watching the stress on members of his family
   C. Ignoring Senator McCarthy's diatribes
   D. Fundraising in 1948

17. HST discovered that "being president is like" what?
   A. "A ringmaster under the big top"
   B. "Riding a tiger. A man has to keep on riding or be swallowed."
   C. "The madam of a whorehouse"
   D. "The father of half-a-dozen misbehaving boys"

18. Eben Ayers, a presidential aide, reported HST's assessment of what figure as "A supreme egoist, who regards himself as something of a god"?
   A. Governor Thomas Dewey of New York
   B. General Douglas MacArthur
   C. Generalissimo Chiang Kai-shek
   D. Chairman Mao Zedong

19. HST, with a keen historical appreciation of the presidency of James K. Polk, said what about interacting with Congress?
    A. "Polk had already done a half-day's work before those rascals in Congress were even stirring."
    B. "Polk thought Congress was always stirring up trouble, no matter who was in the White House."
    C. "Every strong president always has trouble with the Congress, whether there's a war on or not."
    D. "Polk said, 'Ignore 'em!' or perhaps, on occasion, something a little stronger."

20. Why did HST tell Dean Rusk that he admired President James K. Polk?
    A. "The man worked hard to earn his salary."
    B. "Ole Polk didn't give a damn about what anybody thought—well, other than Mrs. Polk."
    C. Polk "regularly told Congress to go to hell on foreign policy matters."
    D. "Polk did his best and then went home to Tennessee and died."

21. Of whom was HST speaking when he told Wallace Graham, "You know, that son-of-a-bitch would get us involved in a war with China"?
    A. Congressman Walter Judd
    B. Senator Joseph McCarthy
    C. Senator Richard Nixon
    D. General Douglas MacArthur

22. After consulting with British Prime Minister Clement Attlee about the potential use of an atomic weapon in Korea, what did HST acknowledge?
    A. "Attlee sure as hell ain't no Winston Churchill!"
    B. "I've worked for peace for five years and six months and it looks like World War III is here."
    C. "There's nothing worse than having a British

prime minister cross the pond to tell me how to be president!"

D. "Attlee is a frustrated old Oxford don who somehow got himself into 10 Downing Street."

23. When Lyndon Johnson became president after John Kennedy's assassination, what did Truman observe?

A. "Boy, do I know what he's thinking and feeling."

B. "At least he won't have to deal with Stalin."

C. "I am sure he won't let us down."

D. "Lyndon Johnson knows how to get things done in Washington."

24. How did HST dismiss caustic, critical press?

A. "The sewer sweepers"

B. "So-called journalists"

C. "Sabotage press"

D. "A pack of dim-witted morons"

25. In 1950, after speaking to the annual meeting of the American Newspaper Guild, HST sobered top aides by observing what about abuse of power by men in public office?

A. "It would only take one bad president to sink our democracy."

B. "I sit and shiver at the thought of what could happen with some demagogue in this office I hold."

C. "You never know what a man will do once he gets here."

D. "Our nation has been spared a demagogue, but I wonder for how much longer."

Observations and Assessments—*Answers*

1. C. "Go to hell!" (Fromkin, 1995, p. 489)
2. C. "More morons than patriots" (Pemberton, 1989, p. 146)
3. B. The "block-headed undertaker" from Nebraska (Hamby, 1995, p. 480)
4. C. "The Striped-pants Boys" (Beschloss, 2007, p. 17; Rockwell, July 8, 1976, p. 17; Walsh, 2005, p. 208)
5. A. "Three amateurs" (Beschloss, 2007, p. 213)
6. B. At a farewell luncheon at Dean Acheson's home (Donovan, 1982, p. 409; Interview with John Snyder, February 17, 1977)
7. C. Limiting the war to the Korean peninsula (Truman, *The New York Times*, January 16, 1953, p. 12)
8. B. "When you lose your own [job]" (Keyes, 2012, p. 32)
9. A. "The president is a glorified public relations man who spends his time flattering, kissing, and kicking people to get them to do what they are supposed to do anyway." (Ferrell, 1980, p. 198)
   B. "It's an all-day and nearly all-night job." (*The New York Times*, February 24, 1952, p. 1E)
   C. "The president has to act for whatever is for the best of the country." (McCoy, 1989, p. 286)
   D. "The man in the White House...represents 150 million people who can't afford a lobby[ist]." (Truman, 1966, 1952–53, p. 657)
10. A. "Nixon is a shifty goddamn liar, and people know it." (Summers, 2000, p. 136)
    B. Nixon has never read the Constitution. "If he has, he doesn't understand it." (Summers, 2000, p. 136)
    D. "Trickie Dickie, the opportunist" (Skidmore, 2004, p. 123)

11. B. Richard Nixon (Truman to Acheson, October 9, 1960)
12. C. "I don't care if his ass hangs out." (Wolz & Hayo, 2012, p. 145)
13. B. "This fellow doesn't know any more about politics than a pig knows about Sunday." (Neal, 2001, p. 290)
14. A. George C. Marshall (Hillman, 1984, p. 219)
15. B. "The most un-American activity in the whole government." (Beschloss, 2000, p. 400)
16. A. Restrictive Secret Service requirements after the assassination attempt (Leuchtenburg, 2015, p. 289)
17. B. "Riding a tiger. A man has to keep on riding or be swallowed." (Whitman, December 27, 1972, p. 46)
18. B. General Douglas MacArthur (Beschloss, 2018, p. 454)
19. C. "Every strong president always has trouble with the Congress, whether there's a war on or not." (Beschloss, 2018, p. 440)
20. C. Polk "regularly told Congress to go to hell on foreign policy matters." (Beschloss, 2018, p. 462)
21. D. General Douglas MacArthur (Beschloss, 2018, p. 470)
22. B. "I've worked for peace for five years and six months and it looks like World War III is here." (Beschloss, 2018, p. 471)
23. C. "I am sure he won't let us down." (Sand, 1993, p. 94)
24. C. "Sabotage press" (Loewenheim, 1989, p. 288)
25. B. "I sit and shiver at the thought of what could happen with some demagogue in this office I hold." (Ferrell, 1991, p. 357)

Independence, Missouri

While the presidential library was under construction, where were HST's offices located?

1. What did the city of Independence do to honor HST becoming president?
   A. Erected a flagpole in the front yard of his home
   B. Named a street for him
   C. Renamed the city auditorium in his honor
   D. Renamed a downtown park for HST

2. HST was surprised by the turnout of Independence citizens to welcome him home on his first visit as president. How did he explain the reaction?
   A. "All these people have seen me two or three times a day, for the last 30 or 40 years. I can't see what there is about me now that would make them turn out like they did today."
   B. "If I had expected this turnout, I would have come home in May."
   C. "I just hope half this many people turn out for my funeral."
   D. "I am still the same Harry Truman who has lived at 219 N. Delaware for 26 years. I haven't change one iota."

3. In September 1945, on a visit home to Independence, why did HST not attend church but stayed home to read "what the papers were saying about him"?
   A. HST was afraid his attendance would create "quite a stir."
   B. HST found it was the only time to read the local papers.
   C. HST did not want to attend the Episcopal Church with Bess and Bess did not want to attend the Baptist Church with HST.
   D. HST had taken an important call from General Marshall that meant he would arrive late and interrupt the service.

4. When election results showed that HST had been elected president in 1948, what did Mayor Roger Sermon do?
   A. Proclaimed a city holiday
   B. Organized a fleet of Cadillac convertibles to bring HST from the Muehlebach Hotel home to Independence
   C. Bought a full page in *The Kansas City Star* to congratulate him
   D. Offered to host the electoral college meeting in Independence

5. For the 1949 inauguration, the Independence Chamber of Commerce raised money for what to honor HST?
   A. An expensive black overcoat with red, white, and blue silk lining
   B. A replica of the Gutenberg Bible on which to place his hand for the oath of office
   C. To rename Van Horn Road, Truman Road
   D. To commission a bust of HST to place in the courthouse

6. Whose funeral was held at 219 N. Delaware?
   A. Bess Wallace Truman
   B. Martha Young Truman
   C. Vietta Garr
   D. Madge Gates Wallace

7. Where were HST's presidential papers initially stored?
   A. Jackson County Courthouse, Kansas City
   B. Vaults at Union National Bank in Kansas City
   C. In limestone caves off Truman Road in Independence
   D. Federal Reserve Bank building in Kansas City

8. While the presidential library was under construction, where were HST's offices located?

A. Federal Reserve Bank building, Kansas City
B. Memorial Building, Independence, Missouri
C. City Hall, Independence, Missouri
D. In his home at 219 N. Delaware

9. On walks in Independence, HST often complimented, "You are doing a good job" to what?

A. An historic gingko tree
B. Independence Court House
C. The city policemen stopping traffic for him
D. City employees picking up trash

10. How did HST summarize his first months in Independence?

A. "Well, after all that 'high-hatting,' I thought I'd better come back to my roots where folks remind you of what is really important."
B. "Well now, I've seen Washington, Paris, New York City, but right here is where I want to be."
C. "There never is and never can be anything like coming back home."
D. "This is the one place I can be just ole Harry."

11. In 1988, when Ronald Reagan campaigned for George H. W. Bush in Independence, Missouri, he declared, "Today Harry Truman's party is the Republican Party." Friends of Truman bought a full-page ad in *The Kansas City Times* that said what?

A. "Aren't you the same Ronald Reagan who campaigned for Harry Truman in 1948?"
B. "Harry Truman voting Republican? Never!"
C. "We knew Harry Truman, Mr. Reagan. And George Bush, as sure as hell, is no Harry Truman."
D. "Harry Truman must be turning over in his grave...."

12. When Lyndon Johnson arrived to greet the Trumans, he tried to explain why he was late. How did Truman respond to the president?
    A. "Presidents never show up anywhere on time."
    B. "It's your own damn fault. If you had left on time, you would have gotten here on time."
    C. "It's time you get a new pilot for that plane."
    D. "Well, I didn't have anything else to do but wait on you."

Independence, Missouri— *Answers*

1. A. Erected a flagpole in the front yard of his home (Taylor, 2013, p. 88)
2. A. "All these people have seen me two or three times a day, for the last 30 or 40 years. I can't see what there is about me now that would make them turn out like they did today." (Taylor, 2013, p. 90)
3. A. HST was afraid his attendance would create "quite a stir." (Taylor, 2013, p. 92)
4. A. Proclaimed a city holiday (Taylor, 2013, p. 96)
5. C. To rename Van Horn Road, Truman Road (Burnes, 2003, p. 193)
6. D. Madge Gates Wallace (Taylor, 2013, p. 105)
7. A. Jackson County Courthouse, Kansas City (McCullough, 1992, p. 930)
8. A. Federal Reserve Bank building, Kansas City (McCullough, 1992, p. 937)
9. A. An historic gingko tree (McCullough, 1992, p. 984)
10. C. "There never is and never can be anything like coming back home." (McCullough, 1992, p. 931)
11. C. "We knew Harry Truman, Mr. Reagan. And George Bush, as sure as hell, is no Harry Truman." (Anthony, June 28, 2012)
12. B. "It's your own damn fault. If you had left on time, you would have gotten here on time." (Beschloss, February 28, 2015)

Religion

What part of the Bible did HST find most meaningful?

1. What did HST do immediately after taking the oath of office in 1945?
   A. Kissed the Gideon Bible
   B. Kissed Mrs. Truman
   C. Wiped tears from his eyes
   D. Asked witnesses to say the Lord's Prayer with him

2. By age 12, what had HST reportedly done?
   A. Memorized the Declaration of Independence
   B. Read the Bible through twice, "cover to cover"
   C. Memorized Jesus's "Sermon on the Mount"
   D. Won the county Latin language competition twice

3. While running for what office did HST say, "If the Almighty God decides that I go there, I am going to pray, as King Solomon did, for wisdom to do the job."
   A. Presiding judge of Jackson County
   B. U.S. Senate
   C. Vice president
   D. President

4. Days after FDR's death, how did HST conclude his first address to Congress?
   A. "I ask for Almighty God's help and your help."
   B. "May God, who directed the steps of Franklin Delano Roosevelt, direct our steps in the coming days."
   C. "I only ask to be a good and faithful servant of my Lord and my people."
   D. "I pray that the God of peace will lead us to the victory that President Franklin D. Roosevelt saw on the horizon."

5. What part of the Bible did HST find most meaningful?
   A. Exodus 20, Deuteronomy 6, Matthew 5–7
   B. Micah
   C. 1 Corinthians 13
   D. Psalm 23

6. Why did HST want to appoint an ambassador to the Vatican?

A. To placate Catholic voters
B. To one-up Cardinal Francis Spellman of New York
C. To unite the moral forces of the world to fight communism
D. To recognize the pope's support of the Allies during World War II

7. HST was *never* a member of which church in the following list?

A. Benton Boulevard Baptist Church, Kansas City, Missouri
B. First Baptist Church, Washington, DC
C. Grand Baptist Church, Grandview, Missouri
D. First Baptist Church, Grandview, Missouri

8. What did HST think was necessary to please God?

A. "Living what you believe."
B. "Living by the Golden Rule every day."
C. "Being baptized in Jesus's name."
D. "What is in the heart and mind is what counts with Almighty God."

9. Why did HST say he was—and remained—a Baptist?

A. "Truth be told, there are lots of Baptist voters in Missouri."
B. "I think that sect gives the common man the shortest and most direct approach to God."
C. "Because of my mother. She was a godly Baptist woman with high moral standards."
D. "Because every so often I need to hear a 'red-hot' sermon by a fired-up preacher who has enough gumption to call sin 'sin'!"

10. Why did HST say he did not attend church regularly?

A. "I cannot appear regularly in church...without feeling like a showpiece or someone on exhibit."
B. "The preachers want to boast, 'I preached to the president last Sunday.'"
C. "If I go, the next Sunday a hundred tourists will show up to take my picture."
D. "Those damn photographers are waiting for me to kneel, to pray, or drop money in the collection plate. They need to hear good preachin' more than anybody but, instead, they focus on me."

11. How did HST describe his religious faith?
    A. "An old-fashioned Bible believin' Baptist"
    B. "A 'light-foot' Baptist"
    C. "A baptized, born-again Baptist"
    D. "A Baptist who thinks 'there's more in acting than in talking.'"

12. What popular American religious leader did Truman ban from the White House?
    A. Norman Vincent Peale
    B. Francis Cardinal Spellman
    C. Monsignor Fulton Sheen
    D. Billy Graham

13. How did HST explain his lack of church attendance on visits back to Independence to the pastor of Grandview Baptist Church?
    A. "I want to be treated as a church member and not the head of a circus."
    B. "I don't want people to come to church to see the president. They ought to go there to worship God."
    C. "I want to sing, pray, listen to the preacher. Not sign autographs on Sunday mornings!"
    D. "Well, I can talk to God just as easily at home as I can in your church house. And God won't take up a collection."

14. What religious group did HST hold in low regard?
    A. Religious counterfeits
    B. Religious fundamentalists
    C. Religious bigots
    D. Religious skeptics

15. HST had a "falling out" with the pastor of the First Baptist Church in Washington, DC, over what issue?
    A. Harry's declining donations to the church
    B. Appointing an ambassador to the Vatican
    C. Federal aid for parochial education
    D. Recognition of Israel

16. HST and Jimmy Carter, as presidents, attended which church in Washington, DC?
    A. The National Cathedral
    B. First Baptist Church
    C. Foundry Methodist Church
    D. Chapel at Walter Reed Hospital

17. HST dismissed religious rivalries between Christians as what?
    A. Foolishness
    B. Pure egotism and foolishness
    C. An unfortunate reality in Christianity
    D. Unworthy of the Constitutional mandate of freedom of religion

18. HST tried to assemble a multidenominational coalition to respond to what?
    A. Communism
    B. Urban poverty
    C. The desegregation of public schools
    D. Weapons of war

19. When HST was sworn in as president on January 20, 1949 he rested his hand on what chapter of the Bible?

A. Psalm 23
B. Exodus 20
C. Matthew 5
D. Micah 4

20. HST claimed that his Good Neighbor Policy originated from what source?
   A. Reading the 10th chapter of the Gospel of Luke
   B. Talking with Prime Minister Winston Churchill
   C. Urging of General George Marshall
   D. A pastor's sermon at First Baptist Church, Washington, DC

21. Why did HST frequently attend services at the chapel of Walter Reed Army Hospital or Bethesda?
   A. Photographers were barred
   B. No offerings were collected
   C. The chaplain was the son of one of Truman's Battery D soldiers
   D. To visit patients afterwards

22. Why did HST believe in reading the Bible?
   A. "The Bible must be read over and over again to get the full meaning out of it."
   B. "Because the more you read it, the more it will stick in your head."
   C. "The Bible is the greatest document in history."
   D. "The moral code set forth in the Bible is unequalled."

23. Besides HST, which of the following presidents were Baptists?
   A. Jimmy Carter
   B. Bill Clinton
   C. Calvin Coolidge
   D. Warren G. Harding

24. What university's awarding HST an honorary doctorate prompted backlash from Southern Baptists?
    A. Brigham Young University
    B. University of Notre Dame
    C. Baylor University
    D. Catholic University of America

25. What did HST say about "religious stuffed shirts"?
    A. "Religious stuffed shirts are just as bad or worse than political ones in my opinion."
    B. "Pay close attention to the man who is both a 'religious stuffed shirt' and a political one."
    C. "They never listen all the way to the end of your sentences."
    D. "They are the present-day Pharisees. So, if the good Lord had to deal with 'em, so do I."

Religion—*Answers*

1. A. Kissed the Gideon Bible (McCullough, 1992, p. 347)
2. B. Read the Bible through twice, "cover to cover" (Yates, 1989, p. 303)
3. B. U.S. Senate (Robbins, 1979, p. 76)
4. C. "I only ask to be a good and faithful servant of my Lord and my people." (Klara, 2010, p. 188)
5. A. Exodus 20, Deuteronomy 6, Matthew 5–7 (Truman, 1953, p. 136)
6. C. To unite the moral forces of the world to fight communism (Kirkendall, 2008, p. 220)
7. B. First Baptist Church, Washington, DC (Bolt, 1992, p. 38)
8. D. "What is in the heart and mind is what counts with Almighty God" (Truman, 1953, p. 131)
9. B. "I think that sect gives the common man the shortest and most direct approach to God." (Yates, 1989, p. 303)
10. A. "I cannot appear regularly in church...without feeling like a showpiece or someone on exhibit." (Truman, 1953, p. 127)
11. D. "A Baptist who thinks 'there's more in acting than in talking.'" (McCullough, 1992, p. 83)
12. D. Billy Graham (Gibbs & Duffy, 2012, p. 20)
13. B. "I don't want people to come to church to see the president. They ought to go there to worship God." (Truman, 1953, p. 127)
14. A. Religious counterfeits (Miller, 1973, p. 363)
15. B. Appointing an ambassador to the Vatican (Jenks, n.d.)
16. B. First Baptist Church (Jenks, n.d.)
17. B. Pure egotism and foolishness (Truman, 1953, p. 132)

18. A. Communism (Truman, 1953, p. 133)
19. B. Exodus 20 (Truman, 1953, p. 135)
20. A. Reading the 10th chapter of the Gospel of Luke (Truman, 1953, p. 139)
21. A. Photographers were barred (Truman, 1953, p. 131)
22. B. "Because the more you read it, the more it will stick in your head." (Truman, 1953, p. 138)
23. A. Jimmy Carter (Grinder & Shaw, 2011, pp. 195–200)
    B. Bill Clinton (Grinder & Shaw, 2011, pp. 211–216)
    D. Warren G. Harding (Grinder & Shaw, 2011, p. 142)
24. C. Baylor University (Holmes, 2012, p. 5; Robbins, 1979, p. 110)
25. A. "Religious stuffed shirts are just as bad or worse than political ones in my opinion." (Robbins, 1979, p. 49)

Post-Presidency

What did HST want to be distinctive about his presidential library?

1. On January 21, 1953, when the Trumans arrived home in Independence, some 20,000 cheering people met them at the railroad station. What did HST say to the crowd?

   A. "I didn't get this many people at some of my rallies in 1948."
   B. "It's a good feeling to be back home."
   C. "I would have come home sooner if I had known you would turn out like this."
   D. "It's late. Why aren't you home in bed?"

2. What was HST's main source of income in the early years of his retirement?

   A. U.S. Senate pension
   B. Director's salary from Ford Motors
   C. Military pension of $112.56 a month
   D. Presidential pension

3. Where did HST do his first interview on the *Today* show in 1953?

   A. On a New York sidewalk as HST stared into a window at the NBC *Today* studio
   B. In his Carlton Hotel suite
   C. In Joey's Coffee Shop in New York City
   D. At the United Nations

4. HST hated to cut the grass at 219 N. Delaware. How did he permanently get out of that chore?

   A. Asked the garage mechanic who worked on his cars
   B. Hired neighborhood boys to cut the grass
   C. Cut the grass on a Sunday morning as neighbors were walking to nearby churches and Bess threw a fit
   D. Paid his brother-in-law

5. What major purchase did HST make immediately after retiring?

A. Central air-conditioning
B. A new Chrysler and a new Dodge
C. The vacant lot next to his house
D. Two television sets

6. What irritated Truman about the public reaction to his announcement that the presidential library would be located in Independence?
   A. Many thought the library was being built with tax money.
   B. "I wish people would stop calling it the Truman Memorial Library. I'm not dead and I feel fine."
   C. "Some of my neighbors complaining the library would cause traffic congestion."
   D. "Republicans are claiming the library will take up valuable park land."

7. What did HST want to be distinctive about his presidential library?
   A. To facilitate the study of the presidency and not just his presidency
   B. Never charge an entrance fee
   C. Sponsor musical concerts
   D. His burial in the courtyard

8. What world leader apologized to HST for misjudging his abilities? "Since 1945 you, more than any other man, have saved Western civilization."
   A. Robert Taft
   B. Sir Winston Churchill
   C. Charles de Gaulle
   D. Dag Hammarskjöld

9. What was HST's net financial profit from writing his presidential memoirs?
   A. Zero—he donated the profits to the Truman Library Institute
   B. $37,000
   C. $267,000
   D. Over $1 million in first 18 months

10. What institution awarded an honorary doctorate in 1956 to *Harricum Truman?*
    A. Harvard University
    B. University of Berlin
    C. Oxford University
    D. University of Missouri

11. When Oxford dignitaries, while conferring an honorary doctorate, declared, "You were the truest of heroes. Direct in your speech and writings, and ever a pattern of simple courage," how did HST respond?
    A. Looked down at the floor
    B. Grinned broadly
    C. Shook his head in humble disagreement
    D. Burst into tears

12. As HST walked through the Oxford campus, students leaned out windows shouting what?
    A. "Give 'em hell, Harricum!"
    B. "Bomb dropper!"
    C. "We're just wild about Harry!"
    D. "Run again!"

13. When did HST and Bess—as a former president and first lady—receive Secret Service protection?
    A. 1953
    B. 1958
    C. 1961
    D. 1963

14. How did HST, in a televised press conference, discredit the forthcoming 1960 Democratic National Convention?
    A. "Rigged"
    B. "Bought by Joseph P. Kennedy"
    C. "Controlled by a bunch of Texas oilmen pushing Lyndon Johnson"

D. "Too dominated by Eleanor Roosevelt's crowd"

15. Before 1960, what had HST concluded about JFK?
    A. "A lazy, ineffective senator who gets too much press"
    B. "Too young and inexperienced"
    C. "Too influenced by ole Joe"
    D. "A young whippersnapper too big for his britches"

16. While campaigning in Texas for JFK in the fall of 1960, HST declared that anyone who would vote for Richard Nixon for president should what?
    A. "Have their heads examined!"
    B. "Should lose the right to vote for eight years."
    C. "Go to hell!"
    D. "Think of Herbert Hoover for an hour or more."

17. When asked why he didn't do something about HST cussing on the campaign trail, who did John Kennedy identify as the only person who could intervene?
    A. Margaret Truman Daniels
    B. Truman's minister
    C. Mrs. Truman
    D. The head of the Democratic National Committee

18. Why did HST *never* visit the White House during the Eisenhower presidency?
    A. He was outraged that Eisenhower installed a putting green off the Oval Office and damaged the floor wearing golf shoes.
    B. Eisenhower never invited him.
    C. He had vowed never to return to the White House until a Democrat was in the Oval Office.
    D. His conviction that "generals never made good presidents."

19. What recognition in Independence did HST and Bess receive in January 1965 from President Lyndon Johnson?
   A. The Congressional Medal of Honor
   B. Medicare cards #1 & #2
   C. The Bronze Star
   D. Presidential Medal of Honor

20. In retirement, HST declined to run for what office?
   A. Supreme Grand Master of American Masons
   B. Governor of Missouri
   C. Secretary General of the United Nations
   D. His old Senate seat

21. HST turned down a $100,000-a-year job requiring him to do what?
   A. Drive only new Ford automobiles
   B. Promote Florida real estate developments
   C. Meet with wealthy clients at Chase Manhattan Bank
   D. Wear only Hart Schaffner Marx suits in public

22. In 1960, how did HST assess his memoirs?
   A. "An insignificant contribution to the study of the presidency."
   B. "My grandchildren's college fund."
   C. "Good God, what crap!"
   D. "Only slightly better than Calvin Coolidge's tome."

23. HST in 1964 became the first former president to address what body?
   A. United Nations
   B. U.S. Senate
   C. National Democratic Convention
   D. Crowd gathered for the lighting of the national Christmas tree

24. Early in 1960 HST supported what Democrat for president?

A. John F. Kennedy
B. Adlai Stevenson
C. Stuart Symington
D. Lyndon B. Johnson

25. HST worked at his library office nearly every day, including weekends. What did he do because he frequently arrived before the staff?
A. Started the coffee
B. Checked the bathrooms for cleanliness
C. Picked up trash on the lawn
D. Answered the phone, gave directions, and answered questions

26. After gall bladder surgery in 1954, how was HST's bill settled at Research Hospital?
A. The hospital offered him a significant discount.
B. The hospital board "wrote off" the cost.
C. HST paid the hospital bill in full himself.
D. Hospital costs were paid by Medicare.

27. When asked why he walked with a cane, HST explained it helped him walk uphill and offered what other reason?
A. "A cane is useful in keeping some dog from peeing on your shoes!"
B. "You can use it to bop on the head of a reporter who asks silly questions."
C. "It makes me look more like a statesman."
D. "Sir Winston Churchill urged me to use a cane. So, I took his advice."

28. What did Bess Truman say when she first saw Thomas Hart Benton's oil painting, "The Old President"?
A. "I see a faint resemblance."
B. "That's him."
C. "Well, it isn't a photograph...."
D. "I never have thought Benton was much of a painter."

29. When asked the secret of his longevity HST answered that walking "keeps those veins in the leg functioning" as does what?
   A. "A little swig of bourbon at breakfast to get the motor revved up"
   B. "Choosing the right grandparents"
   C. "Never sitting up worrying about foolishness"
   D. "Having a wife, daughter, and grandchildren that love you"

30. Why did HST think tourists came to Independence to see him?
   A. "They want to see if I am as ugly as the editorial cartoonists depicted me."
   B. "They've come to see the striped mule of Missouri."
   C. "They want to get a look at an honest politician."
   D. "They want to brag that they shook ole Harry's hand."

31. What was one of first things Bess wanted to do when they returned to Independence?
   A. Take down the five-foot fence around the property
   B. Redo the kitchen
   C. Get active again in her bridge club
   D. Take more Spanish lessons

32. A publisher's representative congratulated Truman for buying and reading so many books saying, "I suppose you read yourself to sleep at night." How did HST respond?
   A. "No, I read to learn the history I don't know."
   B. "Young man, I read all day long."
   C. "No...I like to read myself awake."
   D. "No, I read to find out what the real historians are saying about me."

33. At the dedication of HST's presidential library in

1957, what guest was asked by the White House *not* to attend?

A. Earl Warren
B. Herbert Hoover
C. Eleanor Roosevelt
D. Winston Churchill

34. What did HST say when Mrs. Truman announced she wanted to visit Disneyland?

A. "A fifteen-minute statement" criticizing the idea since everyone knew that Disneyland was "for children"
B. He asked an aide to escort her to the amusement park
C. Instead, he made arrangements to visit the Huntington Library
D. He accompanied Mrs. Truman to Disneyland and "enjoyed himself thoroughly."

35. What was HST's last public responsibility?

A. Addressed the 1964 Democratic National Convention
B. Represented Lyndon Johnson at the funeral of King Paul of Greece in 1964
C. Attended John Kennedy's funeral
D. Attended the dedication of Dwight Eisenhower's presidential library in Abilene, Kansas

36. Invited to attend the 1956 Gridiron Dinner in New York City, why did HST decline?

A. "Nixon will be there if my information is correct. I avoid him like I would avoid a mad dog."
B. "It is already enough of a burden to me to be on the same planet with that man!"
C. "I might say something that would get the Boss mad."
D. "I will not sit at the same table as Richard Nixon."

37. In retirement, what was a constant source of tension between Bess and HST?
   A. Which television show to watch
   B. Harry wanting to drive Bess's car
   C. How fast he drove
   D. The constant stream of visitors by the house

38. In December 1955, HST came home from the office and found Bess burning "stacks of letters" in the fireplace. How did Harry respond?
   A. "So, Bess, we can't afford firewood?"
   B. "Bess, what are you doing? Think of history."
   C. "But I wrote most of those letters...."
   D. "Did Margaret put you up to this?"

Post Presidency—*Answers*

1. B. "It's a good feeling to be back home." (Burnes, 2003, p. 198)
2. C. Military pension of $112.56 a month (McCullough, 1992, p. 928)
3. A. On a New York sidewalk as HST stared into a window at the NBC *Today* studio (Algeo, 2009, p. 158)
4. C. Cut the grass on a Sunday morning as neighbors were walking to nearby churches and Bess threw a fit (Hamby, 1995, p. 627)
5. B. A new Chrysler and a new Dodge (McCullough, 1992, p. 933)
6. B. "I wish people would stop calling it the Truman Memorial Library. I'm not dead and I feel fine." (Burnes, 2003, p. 218)
7. A. To facilitate the study of the presidency and not just his presidency. (Truman, 1953, p. 239).
8. B. Sir Winston Churchill (Sand, 1993, p. 130)
9. B. $37,000 (Hamby, 1995, p. 626)
10. C. Oxford University (McCullough, 1992, p. 952)
11. D. Burst into tears (Skidmore, 2004, p. 125; Ferrell, 1996, pp. 395–396)
12. A. "Give 'em hell, Harricum!" (Skidmore, 2004, p. 126)
13. D. 1963 (McCullough, 1992, p. 982)
14. A. "Rigged" (McCullough, 1992, p. 973)
15. B. "Too young and inexperienced." (Parmet, 1989, p. 198)
16. C. "Go to hell!" (Hamby, 1995, p. 625)
17. C. Mrs. Truman (Hamby, 1995, p. 625; Neal, 2001, p. 214)
18. B. Eisenhower never invited him. (Sand, 1993, p. 77)
19. B. Medicare cards #1 & #2 (McCullough, 1992, p. 984)
20. D. His old Senate seat (Truman, 1953, p. 123)

21. B. Promote Florida real estate developments (McCullough, 1992, p. 929)

22. C. "Good God, what crap!" (McCullough, 1992, p. 937)

23. B. U.S. Senate (McCullough, 1992, p. 983)

24. C. Stuart Symington (McCullough, 1992, p. 971)

25. D. Answered the phone, gave directions, and answered questions (McCullough, 1992, pp. 966–967)

26. C. HST paid the bill in full himself (Truman, 1963, p. 104)

27. B. "You can use it to bop on the head of a reporter who asks silly questions." (Failing health, December 26, 1972, p. 5)

28. B. "That's him." (Burnes, 2003, p. 191)

29. B. "Choosing the right grandparents." (Failing health, December 26, 1972, p. 5)

30. B. "They've come to see the striped mule of Missouri." (Burnes, 2003, p. 191)

31. A. Take down the five-foot fence around the property (Burnes, 2003, p. 190)

32. C. "No...I like to read myself awake." (McCullough in Zinsser, 1986, p. 33)

33. B. Herbert Hoover (Gibbs & Duffy, 2012, p. 97)

34. A. "A fifteen-minute statement" criticizing the idea since everyone knew that Disneyland was "for children" (Truman, 1973, p. 565)

35. B. Represented Lyndon Johnson at the funeral of King Paul of Greece in 1964 (Beschloss, 1997, pp. 269–270; Sand, 1993, p. 109)

36. D. "I will not sit at the same table as Richard Nixon." (Truman-Nixon Chill, February 23, 1986)

37. C. How fast he drove (Algeo, 2009, pp. 42–43)

38. B. "Bess, what are you doing? Think of history." (Daniel, 2011, p. xii)

Harry "Being Harry"

What did HST often call his poker buddies in Independence?

1. HST, mistakenly, thought he was distantly related to what U.S. president?
   A. William Henry Harrison
   B. John Tyler
   C. William McKinley
   D. William Howard Taft

2. HST rarely made campaign speeches on what day of the week?
   A. Sunday
   B. Saturday
   C. Tuesday
   D. Thursday

3. What song did HST dislike particularly when Richard Nixon played a few bars on a piano in the Truman Library?
   A. "God Bless America"
   B. "The Missouri Waltz"
   C. "This Land Is Your Land"
   D. "Yankee Doodle"

4. On the campaign trail, how could HST judge the age of a horse/mule?
   A. By examining the hooves and calves
   B. By listening to the animal's heartbeat
   C. By examining the animal's teeth
   D. By what he called "a farmer's sense"

5. In posing for photographs with friends, what did HST often do "to keep SOBs from cropping people out of my photos"?
   A. Crossed arms with friends
   B. Asked friends to squeeze in close
   C. Turned sideways
   D. Made photographers promise not to crop out anyone

6. About what did HST brag?
   A. That he had proved the pollsters wrong in '48
   B. That he walked almost every day
   C. That he had maintained his waistline and wore suits he had worn in 1935
   D. That Bess had been the only woman he had ever loved

7. HST, when irritated, would pen stinging letters to settle scores with adversaries but rarely mailed them. What did his staff call these letters?
   A. "Pants scorchers"
   B. The "I guess I really told him!" letters
   C. "He wouldn't dare send this!" communications
   D. "Longhand spasms"

8. Where did HST have his first meal as president?
   A. In the White House mess
   B. Dave's Diner near the White House
   C. At a neighbor's kitchen table
   D. In the secretary of state's dining room

9. What did HST often call his poker buddies in Independence?
   A. The Harpie Club
   B. The Knights of the Round Chips
   C. The Bourbon Dynasty
   D. The Old Sons of Independence

10. Why did HST prefer poker over other games for relaxation?
    A. Truman needed male comradery
    B. Truman loved to "clean out" players' wallets
    C. Truman could relax
    D. Truman loved to test his psychological assumptions of other players

11. Why did HST want his steak "well done"?
    A. "Only coyotes and predatory animals eat raw beef."
    B. "I never want a steak on my plate to say, 'Moo.'"
    C. "I wanted to make certain that Republican cattlemen were not trying to poison me."
    D. "That's the way Teddy Roosevelt ate steak!"

12. HST corresponded over the years with what Hollywood personality?
    A. Henry Fonda
    B. Jimmy Stuart
    C. Groucho Marx
    D. John Wayne

13. Why did HST complain about being lonely in the White House?
    A. Bess and Margaret were away in Independence for long periods of time
    B. He let the staff leave at 6:00 p.m.
    C. Few guests were comfortable without Bess Truman being present
    D. He had no one to play piano duets with

14. How did HST describe Paul Hume, the music critic for trashing Margaret's debut in Washington's Constitution Hall?
    A. "That crotchety old deaf fool!"
    B. "An eight-ulcer man on four-ulcer pay."
    C. "A nincompoop who can't sing a note."
    D. "A sissy who doesn't know the difference between classical music and hillbilly music!"

15. HST claimed that he never had trouble doing what?
    A. Firing an insubordinate or incompetent person
    B. Falling asleep at night
    C. Sailing on open seas
    D. Trimming fat in the federal budget

16. Years after Margaret's debut, what transpired when music critic Paul Hume visited the Truman Library?
    A. The men attended a concert in Kansas City together.
    B. Truman accompanied Hume at the piano when Hume sang to the office staff.
    C. Truman asked Hume to sign a framed copy of the review.
    D. Truman gave Hume an hour-long tour of the library.

17. What was HST's favorite dessert?
    A. Apple pie with vanilla ice cream
    B. Angel food cake
    C. Peach cobbler a la mode
    D. Chocolate ice cream with butterscotch sauce

18. When HST vacationed in Key West he played a lot of poker. What phrase did the press secretary use to camouflage this activity from the public?
    A. "The president spent the evening reviewing potential world 'hot' spots."
    B. "The president spent the evening visiting with friends on the south porch."
    C. "The president spent the evening plowing through stacks of correspondence and magazines."
    D. "The president relaxed by listening to favorite music."

19. While vacationing in Key West, Florida, HST often wore "Truman shirts." What were "Truman shirts"?
    A. Oxford-cloth shirts meant to be worn without ties
    B. Bright Hawaiian shirts
    C. Short-sleeve heavily starched white dress shirts
    D. Guayaberas, Cuban-made linen sports shirts

20. How many bow ties did Harry own?
    A. Less than a dozen at any one time
    B. At least one from each state
    C. Over 200
    D. Over 400

21. HST wept as what leader was dying?
    A. General George Marshall
    B. Mayor Fiorello La Guardia
    C. General John J. Pershing
    D. King George VI of England

22. HST disliked what category of jokes?
    A. Traveling salesman
    B. Loose women
    C. Mother-in-law
    D. Politicians

23. What former president had HST's highest appreciation?
    A. Franklin D. Roosevelt
    B. Theodore Roosevelt
    C. Woodrow Wilson
    D. Andrew Jackson

24. On 11 occasions when HST vacationed in Key West, where did the president often stay?
    A. La Concha Hotel
    B. A private house leased by the government
    C. A navy submarine base
    D. Bernard Baruch's vacation cottage

25. Where was a beach was *renamed* for HST?
    A. Key West, Florida
    B. Jackson County, Missouri
    C. Berlin, West Germany
    D. Branson, Missouri

26. Why did Harry fire Henrietta Nesbitt, the White House housekeeper?
    A. She overcooked vegetables
    B. She refused to serve biscuits and gravy for his breakfast
    C. She was condescending to the Trumans and ignored Bess's meal requests
    D. She expected meals to be eaten in 30 minutes

27. Who cooked for the Trumans in Independence and, over time, became an extended member of the family?
    A. Lilly Smith
    B. Mamie Mae Rice
    C. Vietta Garr
    D. Francis Porter

28. HST was the first president to watch what event on TV?
    A. Vladmir Horowitz playing Tchaikovsky's Piano Concerto No. 1 in B♭ minor
    B. Coverage of the Democratic National Convention
    C. The final game of the 1948 World Series
    D. The first paid telecast for a presidential candidate

29. What item that would *never* have been served HST at breakfast?
    A. One egg
    B. One strip of bacon
    C. Biscuits and gravy
    D. Skimmed milk

30. Why did HST walk a mile-and-a-half at a pace of 120 paces per minute?
    A. "That pace keeps those reporters following me sweating."
    B. "Safest exercise for a man my age."
    C. "Keeps me from going to flab like some folks in Washington."
    D. "Gives your whole body a vigorous workout."

31. HST's joked that his early ambition was to be either a politician or what?
    A. Military officer
    B. Piano player in a whorehouse
    C. A private detective
    D. Lawyer

32. What was the title of the first book HST wrote?

    A. *Memoirs*
    B. *Drunken Sailor: How the Nation's Defense Contractors Waste Taxpayers' Money*
    C. *Results of County Planning*
    D. *The Farmer Gets a New Deal*

33. In 1964, why did HST turn down a $50,000 TV network contract to be a commentator at the Democratic National Convention?

    A. "Bess said I would not be able to keep from cussing 'while commentating' on the air."
    B. "They didn't want me; they wanted the presidency."
    C. "I preferred offering commentary at the Republican National Convention."
    D. "By this point I had had my fill of political conventions."

34. How much bourbon did HST say he drank in a day?

    A. "Not as much as some politicians I could name."
    B. "Only enough to get my motor revved up."
    C. "Two ounces."
    D. "As much as I damn please."

35. What did HST say about money in politics?

    A. "I always had enough money to run a campaign in Jackson County."
    B. "I never had enough money to run a statewide campaign for the Senate."
    C. "I did not have enough money to run a campaign for the presidency."
    D. "After most campaigns, I ended up with money in the bank."

36. What did HST say about his reading habits?

    A. "I read a great deal, but not as much as I want to."
    B. "I read a great deal more than most presidents."

C. "I read a great deal, but not as much as Mrs. Truman."

D. "I read a great deal more than most members of Congress."

37. Who did HST consider a "100 percent American"?

   A. "Every citizen of the Republic who is willing to do his part in defending it when it is in danger."

   B. "That individual who votes, pays his taxes, serves on juries."

   C. "The inhabitants of the United States at the time the European settlers waded ashore."

   D. "That individual who fully embraces the American Creed: liberty and justice for all."

38. What action did HST take after discovering liquor was disappearing at Blair House?

   A. HST had FBI agents interview staff and take fingerprints.

   B. HST had locks installed on the cabinets.

   C. HST filled several bottles with vinegar.

   D. HST filled several bottles with water.

39. After receiving an autographed copy of Jonathan Daniels's book, *Man of Independence*, Eben Ayers apologized for troubling HST for his autograph. How did HST respond?

   A. "Hell, what's one more signature in the course of a day!"

   B. "I have to sign my name for so many sons-of-bitches that it is a pleasure to sign it for someone I like."

   C. "You are going to read it, aren't you?"

   D. "I better not find out that you sold this masterpiece to a used bookstore!"

40. How many canes did HST estimate owning?
    A. A couple dozen
    B. At least 50
    C. 100 or so
    D. "Well, more than I can use in a single day."

41. What particularly pleased Truman about the building of his presidential library?
    A. It did not cost Jackson County taxpayers one cent.
    B. The trustees raised an endowment fund in excess of $1 million.
    C. All the building materials were from Missouri.
    D. There would never be an admission fee.

42. About what syndicated columnist did HST complain saying, "Whenever I get my information from [him] I hope someone will have my head examined—I'll need it."?
    A. Lowell Thomas
    B. Walter Lipman
    C. Westbrooke Pegler
    D. Drew Pearson

43. Why did HST resent Richard Nixon?
    A. Nixon wasted time in Congress looking under rocks for Communists.
    B. Nixon repeatedly lied about the Truman administration.
    C. Truman believed Nixon had called him a traitor during the 1952 campaign.
    D. Nixon put HST's piano in storage.

44. Asked if he sang tenor or baritone, how did HST respond?
    A. "Well, it depends on what I am singing."
    B. "I never sing...I'm saddest when I sing and so are those that listen to me."
    C. "I sing so softly that no one can hear."
    D. "Tenor."

45. Before leaving the White House, how did HST verbalize his potential for being assassinated?
    A. "Well, if someone wants a little exercise I will give him more than he expected!"
    B. "If any nut tries to shoot me, I'll take the pistol away from him, ram it down his throat and pull the trigger."
    C. "I will use my cane on the man's head like ole Andy Jackson did on his assailant's head."
    D. "If anyone accosts me he'll wish he had never tried! If he tries to accost Mrs. Truman he won't be alive to remember."

46. HST once said there were rules that he followed as a politician, "win, lose, or draw." Which of the following did he mention?
    A. Never handle political money
    B. Refuse gifts and favors
    C. Make no speeches for money while holding national office
    D. Never touch a drop of liquor until after a speech

Harry "Being Harry"
—Answers

1. B. John Tyler (McCullough, 1992, p. 355)
2. A. Sunday (White, 2014, p. 159)
3. B. "The Missouri Waltz" (Summers, 2000, p. 499)
4. C. By examining the animal's teeth (White, 2014, p. 150; McCullough, 1992, p. 679)
5. A. Crossed arms with friends (Wolz & Hayo, 2012, p. 148)
6. C. That he had maintained his waistline and wore suits he had worn in 1935 (Hamby, 1995, p. 467)
7. D. "Longhand spasms" (McCullough, 1992, p. 480)
8. C. At a neighbor's kitchen table (Hedley, 1979, p. 31)
9. A. The Harpie Club (Burnes, 2003, p. 150)
10. C. Truman could relax (Burnes, 2003, p. 150)
11. A. "Only coyotes and predatory animals eat raw beef." (Truman, 1953, p. 84)
12. C. Groucho Marx (Geselbracht, 2001, pp. 46–50)
13. A. Bess and Margaret were away in Independence for long periods of time. (McCullough, 1992, p. 750)
14. B. "An eight-ulcer man on four-ulcer pay" (Truman, 1973, p. 502)
15. B. Falling asleep at night (Truman, 1953, p. 264)
16. D. Truman gave Hume an hour-long tour of the library. (McCullough, 1992, p. 975)
17. B. Angel food cake (Taylor, 2013, p. 86)
18. B. "The president spent the evening visiting with friends on the south porch." (Knutson, 2014, p. 256)
19. B. Bright Hawaiian shirts (Knutson, 2014, p. 254)
20. D. Over 400 (Schneider, October 23, 2013)
21. A. General George Marshall (McCullough, 1992, p. 970)

22. C. Mother-in-law (Beschloss, May 8, 2014)

23. D. Andrew Jackson (Truman, 1989, p. 272)

24. C. A navy submarine base (Yates, 1989, p. 200)

25. A. Key West, Florida (Wolz & Hayo, 2012, p. 126)

26. C. She was condescending to the Trumans and ignored Bess's meal requests. (Truman, 1973, p. 246)

27. C. Vietta Garr (Burnes, 2003, pp. 204–205)

28. B. Coverage of the Democratic National Convention (McCullough, 1992, p. 637)

29. C. Biscuits and gravy (Truman, January 3, 1952; Walsh, 2005, p. 112)

30. D. "Gives your whole body a vigorous workout." (Truman, 1953, p. 87)

31. B. Piano player in a whorehouse (Hamilton, 2010, p. 47)

32. C. *Results of County Planning* (Pemberton, 1989, p. 184)

33. B. "They didn't want me; they wanted the presidency." (Sand, 1993, p. 127)

34. C. "Two ounces." (Truman, 1953, p. 96)

35. C. "I did not have enough money to run a campaign for the presidency." (Truman, 1953, p. 152)

36. A. "I read a great deal, but not as much as I want to." (Truman, 1953, p. 163)

37. C. "The inhabitants of the United States at the time the European settlers waded ashore." (Truman, 1953, p. 175)

38. B. HST had locks installed on the cabinets. (Ferrell, 1991, p. 344)

39. B. "I have to sign my name for so many sons-of-bitches that it is a pleasure to sign it for someone I like." (Ferrell, 1991, p. 388)

40. C. 100 or so (Algeo, 2009, p. 23)

41. A. It did not cost Jackson County taxpayers one cent. (Hedley, 1979, p. 253)

42. D. Drew Pearson (Truman, 2004, p. 335)

43. C. Truman believed Nixon had called him a traitor during the 1952 campaign. (Frank, 2013, p. 258)

44. B. "I never sing...I'm saddest when I sing and so are those that listen to me." (Spann & Williams, 2008, p. 224; Kirk, 1986, p. 254)

45. B. "If any nut tries to shoot me, I'll take the pistol away from him, ram it down his throat and pull the trigger." (Beschloss, 2018, p. 437)

47. C. Make no speeches for money while holding national office (Dunar, 1989, p. 149)

Truman on His Contemporaries

Who told HST, "Have confidence in yourself. If you do not, the people will lose confidence in you."?

1. Before meeting Winston Churchill at Potsdam, what did HST say about the prime minister of Great Britain?
   A. "Mr. Churchill always wants to get his way."
   B. "Rumor has it that that man drinks more than I do...."
   C. "I am sure we can get along if he doesn't try to give me too much soft soap."
   D. "Churchill is not going to drive me nuts the way he did FDR!"

2. Before traveling to their first meeting in Potsdam, what did HST tell aides about Josef Stalin?
   A. "He is straightforward. Knows what he wants and will compromise when he can't get it."
   B. "I can deal with Stalin. The question is: Can he deal with me?"
   C. "People who disagree with him seem to disappear."
   D. "His bark is not nearly as loud as some Republicans in the U.S. Senate."

3. What contemporary did HST not mention in his memoirs?
   A. John J. Pershing
   B. Jimmy Roosevelt
   C. Tom Pendergast
   D. Richard Nixon

4. In September 1959, HST played a duet on television with what well-known comedian?
   A. Bob Hope
   B. Milton Berle
   C. Jack Benny
   D. Arthur Godfrey

5. HST dismissed President Eisenhower as...?
   A. "The bonehead in the White House"
   B. "The First Golfer"

214

C. "A man who couldn't do anything except issue orders"

D. "Pinheaded," "chickenhearted," "a surly, angry, and disagreeable man"

6. Although Speaker Sam Rayburn and HST often shared bourbon on late afternoons in the speaker's private office, on occasion how did Rayburn challenge his friend?

A. "Harry, you ain't got the hand to win the jackpot this time."

B. "Mr. President, as a southern Democrat, can I tell you why you might want to rethink that."

C. "Now, Mr. President, let's consider that."

D. "Mr. President, I think you could use another bourbon before you agree to that!"

7. What HST-appointed Supreme Court justice continued to advise him and was part of the president's inner circle?

A. Thomas Clark

B. Harold Burton

C. Frederick Vinson

D. Sherman Minton

8. How did HST describe Secretary of State Edward Stettinius, Jr.—an FDR holdover who served briefly in the Truman cabinet?

A. "An ignoramus when it comes to European history."

B. "As dumb as they come."

C. "A man who didn't have enough sense to pour piss out of a boot."

D. "An old horse who should have been put out to pasture years ago."

9. To whom was HST referring when he said, "He didn't know shit from apple butter"?

A. Joseph McCarthy, senator from Wisconsin
B. Henry Morgenthau, treasury secretary
C. Thomas Dewey, Republican presidential candidate in 1948
D. Drew Pearson, syndicated columnist

10. HST refused "to spend hours and hours" talking with what "old goat"?

A. Entrepreneur Bernard Baruch
B. Ambassador Joseph Kennedy
C. Justice Felix Frankfurter
D. Senator Arthur Vandenberg

11. What national labor leader did HST boast he would not appoint "chief dogcatcher of this country"?

A. Walter Reuther
B. John L. Lewis
C. Philip Murray
D. David Dubinsky

12. Who did HST call a SOB for saying "...[he] thinks he can cause any of these people to be discharged by me by some smart-aleck statement over the air or in the paper?"

A. Roy Roberts, *The Kansas City Star*
B. Drew Pearson, syndicated columnist
C. Walter Winchell, syndicated columnist
D. H. V. Kaltenborn, syndicated columnist

13. Who warned HST, "The special interests and the sycophants...will tell you you're the greatest man alive—but you and I know you ain't."?

A. Eddie Jacobson
B. Bess Truman
C. Former vice president John Nance Garner
D. Speaker Sam Rayburn

14. To whom did HST confess, "I'm not big enough. I'm not big enough for this job!"?
    A. Senator George Aiken
    B. Bess Truman
    C. Eleanor Roosevelt
    D. Harry Hopkins

15. Who told HST, "Have confidence in yourself. If you do not, the people will lose confidence in you."?
    A. Eleanor Roosevelt
    B. Speaker Sam Rayburn
    C. Senate Majority Leader Alben Barkley
    D. Bess Truman

16. At Potsdam, what did HST and Prime Minister Clement Attlee do for relaxation?
    A. Played poker late into the night
    B. Sang bawdy songs from World War I
    C. Drained a bottle of bourbon while talking
    D. Walked for an hour each morning

17. Traveling by train to Fulton, Missouri, for a speech, Churchill asked the president if he would mind if he called him "Harry." How did HST answer?
    A. "No, Winston."
    B. "Do you call the king by his first name?"
    C. "What did you call President Roosevelt?"
    D. "I've been called every thing under the sun so it doesn't really matter."

Truman on His Contemporaries
—*Answers*

1. C. "I am sure we can get along if he doesn't try to give me too much soft soap." (Hamby, 1995, p. 328)

2. A. "He is straightforward. Knows what he wants and will compromise when he can't get it." (Hamby, 1995, p. 331)

3. D. Richard Nixon (Hoff-Wilson, 1989, p. 257)

4. C. Jack Benny (Johnson, 1999, p. 110)

5. D. "Pinheaded," "chickenhearted," "a surly, angry, and disagreeable man." (Hamby, 1995, p. 621)

6. C. "Now, Mr. President, let's consider that." (Champagne, 1989, p. 295)

7. C. Frederick Vinson (Murphy, 1989, p. 381)

8. B. "As dumb as they come." (Neiberg, 2016, p. 33)

9. B. Henry Morgenthau, treasury secretary (McCullough, 1992, p. 404)

10. A. Entrepreneur Bernard Baruch (McCullough, 1992, p. 546)

11. B. John L. Lewis (Harrison, 2006, p. 324)

12. B. Drew Pearson, syndicated columnist (McCullough, 1992, p. 737)

13. D. Speaker Sam Rayburn (Dorough, 1962, p. 368)

14. A. Senator George Aiken (Baime, 2017, p. 124)

15. C. Senate Majority Leader Alben Barkley (McCullough, 1992, p. 356)

16. B. Sang bawdy songs from World War I (Hamilton, 2010, p. 85)

17. A. "No, Winston." (Ferrell, 1991, p. 348)

Christmas

What two things were distinctive about the first Truman Christmas in the White House in 1945?

1. What year(s) did HST *not* spend Christmas in Independence?
   A. 1945
   B. 1947
   C. 1950
   D. 1952

2. On Christmas Eve 1950, what did HST help dedicate?
   A. First Baptist Church, Grandview, Missouri
   B. First Baptist Church, Washington, DC
   C. First Baptist Church, Independence, Missouri
   D. First Presbyterian Church, Independence, Missouri

3. When HST returned to Independence for Christmas 1948, what did he do for reporters?
   A. Held a press conference in front of the family's Christmas tree
   B. Organized the "Truman Walking Club" for reporters who thought they could keep up with him on his morning walks
   C. Stirred up a large batch of his legendary bourbon eggnog
   D. Announced that he would make no announcements on Christmas so reporters could "take the day off"

4. What was Truman's favorite Christmas carol?
   A. "Joy to the World"
   B. "Silent Night"
   C. "Away in a Manger"
   D. "O Little Town of Bethlehem"

5. Why did HST and Bess intensely argue during Christmas 1945?
   A. His delay getting home for Christmas
   B. His invitation to Battery D members to visit 219 N. Delaware Street for a cup of Christmas spirit

C. HST's commitment to play poker on Christmas eve with friends

D. How much money he spent on gifts for Margaret

6. On Christmas Eve 1948, from where did HST light the national Christmas tree?
   A. From the Oval Office
   B. From the Little White House in Key West
   C. From Independence
   D. From the south portico of the White House

7. In what year was HST's speech for lighting the national Christmas tree taped?
   A. 1946
   B. 1948
   C. 1950
   D. 1952

8. What two things were distinctive about the first Truman Christmas in the White House in 1945?
   A. Santa Claus and three cabinet members arrived on the White House grounds in a sleigh.
   B. The East Room had no Christmas tree.
   C. Ten thousand people were admitted to the White House grounds for the lighting of the national tree.
   D. Cabinet members and spouses served Christmas punch to those attending.

9. What special project did Head Usher Alonzo Fields supervise each Christmas for HST?
   A. Lighting of the national tree
   B. Selecting a needy African American family and a needy Caucasian family to receive a Christmas turkey and presents (Seeley, 1996, p. 56)
   C. Decorating the White House
   D. Buying gifts for the White House staff

10. Why, during Christmas 1945, did *The New York Times* and *The Washington Post* criticize HST?
   A. For not expediting bringing more soldiers home from Europe for Christmas with families
   B. For not giving federal employees an extra day off because Christmas fell on Sunday
   C. For "taking chances with his personal safety" and the safety of the crew by flying home to Independence in dangerous weather
   D. For disrupting the holidays of the families of White House staff who had accompanied HST to Independence

11. Given that American troops were on the ground in Korea at Christmas 1950, HST called upon Americans to do what?
   A. For churches to make Christmas "special" for families of military deployed in Korea
   B. For Americans to renew their faith in God
   C. For Americans to make sacrificial gifts to charities engaged in caring for Korean refugees
   D. For a national day of prayer for peace in Korea

12. Where did HST spend his last Christmas?
   A. In Key West, Florida
   B. In Research Hospital, Kansas City
   C. In New York City with Margaret's family
   D. In Maui, Hawaii

Christmas—*Answers*

1. B. 1947 (Zobrist, 1989, p. 171)
   D. 1952 (Zobrist, 1989, p. 171)
2. A. First Baptist Church, Grandview, Missouri (Truman, 1950, pp. 758–759)
3. B. Organized the "Truman Walking Club" for reporters who thought they could keep up with him on his morning walks (Taylor, 2013, p. 98)
4. B. "Silent Night" (Spann & Williams, 2008, p. 226)
5. A. His delay getting home for Christmas (Angelo, 2005, p. 89)
6. C. From Independence (Seeley, 1996, p. 61)
7. C. 1950 (Seeley, 1996, p. 63)
8. B. The East Room had no Christmas tree. (Seeley, 1996, p. 55)
   C. Ten thousand people were admitted to the White House grounds for the lighting of the national tree. (Seeley, 1996, p. 56)
9. B. Selecting a needy African American family and a needy Caucasian family to receive a Christmas turkey and presents (Seeley, 1996, p. 56)
10. C. For "taking chances with his personal safety" and the safety of the crew by flying home to Independence in dangerous weather (Seeley, 1996, p. 57)
11. B. For Americans to renew their faith in God (Seeley, 1996, p. 63)
12. B. In Research Hospital, Kansas City (McCullough, 1992, p. 988)

Money

What financial transaction did HST have to take before returning home to Independence in 1953?

1. HST—hoping to build up a nest egg for marriage—lost $7,500 in September 1916 in what business venture?
   A. Speculating on Kansas farmland
   B. In a lead and zinc mine in Oklahoma
   C. In drilling in oil fields in southern Missouri
   D. A horse racing track near Belton, Missouri

2. For how much did HST, in 1919, sell his interest in the family's Grandview farm?
   A. $2,500
   B. $5,500
   C. $10,000
   D. $15,000

3. Why did Truman & Jacobson Haberdashery go bankrupt?
   A. The post-World War I economic bust
   B. They did not sell under-the-counter whiskey
   C. A clerk was stealing from the cash register
   D. Truman's taste in clothes to sell was too extravagant for customers

4. After Truman & Jacobson Haberdashery closed in 1922, HST never declared bankruptcy. When did he liquidate his debt?
   A. 1927
   B. 1929
   C. 1935
   D. 1944

5. Early in marriage, HST had financial success selling what?
   A. Farms in eastern Jackson County
   B. Kansas City Auto Club memberships
   C. Rifles and shotguns at gun shows
   D. Horses, donkeys, and mules

6. HST yearly earned $10,000 as a senator—a considerable sum during the Depression. Which of the following was *not* a factor in finances always being tight for the Trumans?
   A. The Trumans maintained residences in Independence and in Washington.
   B. Truman spent large amounts of his own money on his campaigns.
   C. Truman had financial responsibilities for his widowed mother and unmarried sister.
   D. Truman was still paying down debts from the failure of the haberdashery.

7. What did HST write Bess after Boss Pendergast went to federal prison?
   A. "Looks like everybody got rich in Jackson County but me."
   B. "I'm glad I can still sleep well even if it is a hardship on you... for me to be so damn poor."
   C. "I am afraid the Boss won't live out his sentence."
   D. "He should have appealed his conviction."

8. What financial transaction did HST have to take before returning home to Independence in 1953?
   A. Signed a contract to write his memoirs
   B. Borrowed against his Social Security
   C. Sold 100 acres of his family's Grandview farm
   D. Borrowed money from the National Bank in Washington "to tide them over"

9. HST estimated that between early 1953 and November 1958, he spent how much of his own money maintaining an office and a small staff?
   A. $ 75,375
   B. $104,300
   C. $153,000
   D. "Too damn much!"

10. How did HST avoid "financial embarrassment" as an ex-president?
    A. Sold some farmland inherited from his mother
    B. Served on three corporate boards
    C. Offered informal advice on foreign investments to wealthy Kansas Citians
    D. Accepted small donations from wealthy friends

11. Because of high taxes paid on intellectual property, i.e., his memoirs, what tax rate did HST pay?
    A. 25.9 %
    B. 36 %
    C. 51 %
    D. 67.5 %

12. HST did not receive a pension for the first years of his ex-presidency until Congress passed a bill to provide for former presidents. How much was the original pension?
    A. $25,000 total
    B. $25,000 personal plus $50,000 for maintaining an office
    C. $75,000 in a lump-sum check paid at the first of the year
    D. Amount determined annually by Congress

13. HST and Bess never owned a house until what year?
    A. 1953, when they bought out her siblings' interests in Madge Wallace's estate
    B. 1956 when HST sold farmland in Grandview
    C. 1954 when wealthy friends bought the house and signed the deed over to the Trumans
    D. 1946 from the first advance for his *Memoirs*

14. What was an underlying principle about HST's poker games?
    A. "Nobody would get hurt if his luck or his skill was bad."
    B. "You win some, you lose some but you *never* complain."
    C. "You always play better poker with good bourbon."
    D. "No one is going to the poor house after playing poker with me!"

15. How much did HST's presidential library in Independence, Missouri, cost to build in 1950s dollars?
    A. $1.8 million
    B. $2.5 million
    C. $4.3 million
    D. $5.1 million

Money—*Answers*

1. B. In a lead and zinc mine in Oklahoma (Johnson, 1989, p. 129)

2. D. $15,000 (Johnson, 1989, p. 129)

3. A. The post-World War I economic bust (Bickerton, 1989, p. 185)

4. C. 1935 (Johnson, 1989, p. 129)

5. B. Kansas City Auto Club memberships (Johnson, 1989, p. 129)

6. C. Truman had financial responsibilities for his widowed mother and unmarried sister. (Johnson, 1989, p. 128)

7. A. "Looks like everybody got rich in Jackson County but me." (Ferrell, 1983, p. 426)

   B. "I'm glad I can still sleep well even if it is a hardship on you...for me to be so damn poor." (Brinkley & Dyer, 2004, p. 367; Johnson, 1989, p. 129)

8. D. Borrowed money from the National Bank in Washington "to tide them over" (Skidmore, 2004, pp. 121, 928)

9. C. $153,000 (Johnson, 1989, p. 129)

10. A. Sold some farmland inherited from his mother (Johnson, 1989, p. 129)

11. D. 67.5 % (Johnson, 1989, p. 129)

12. B. $25,000 personal plus $50,000 for maintaining an office (Johnson, 1989, p. 129)

13. A. 1953, when they bought out her siblings' interests in Madge Wallace's estate (Algeo, 2009, p. 20; Robbins, 1979, p. 53)

14. A. "Nobody would get hurt if his luck or his skill was bad." (Knutson, 2014, p. 265)

15. A. $1.8 million (McCullough, 1992, p. 961)

End of Life

Why did HST say he wanted to be buried in the library courtyard?

1. How did HST, who left office with low poll ratings, say he hoped to be judged for his presidency?
   A. "I don't know what history will say about me. But I can honestly say I did the best I could."
   B. "No president can be accurately evaluated during his term in office."
   C. "I trust the judgment of the American people."
   D. "I did my best of my ability to preserve, protect, and defend the Constitution from all enemies, foreign and domestic."

2. What triggered HST's health decline in 1964?
   A. A mild stroke
   B. A fall in the bathroom which cracked a couple of ribs and cut his head
   C. A severe prostate infection
   D. A heart attack

3. What did HST exclaim after reviewing plans for his funeral?
   A. "Good God, this is going to cost a fortune!"
   B. "It looks like a damn fine show...I just hate that I won't be around to see it."
   C. "This wears me out just reading this document."
   D. "Going through all this ceremony will be too hard on Mrs. Truman."

4. Why was there no eulogy?
   A. The eulogist became ill just before the service began.
   B. HST believed that a person's life should speak for itself.
   C. The family wanted to keep the service brief for Bess's sake.
   D. Margaret Truman Daniel nixed the eulogy an hour before the service.

5. Upon HST's death in 1972, who altered the original funeral plans to avoid a lying-in-state in Washington?
   A. The Secret Service
   B. The Trustees of the Truman Library
   C. Bess Truman
   D. Margaret Truman Daniel

6. Where in Independence was HST's funeral held on December 28, 1972?
   A. Auditorium, Community of Christ
   B. Sanctuary, First Baptist Church
   C. Auditorium, Independence High School
   D. Auditorium, Truman Library

7. Where in Key West was a special memorial service conducted for HST?
   A. Auditorium of Key West High School
   B. Truman Beach
   C. St. Mary's Episcopal Church
   D. The Chapel, Naval Air Station

8. Why did HST say he wanted to be buried in the library courtyard?
   A. "Convenience for people who come to the library"
   B. "I want to be out there so I can get up and walk into my office if I want to."
   C. "Well, Bess claims, I still want to be the center of attention."
   D. "If it's there, it has to be plain."

9. Who is *not* buried at the Truman Presidential Library?
   A. Harry Truman
   B. Bess Truman
   C. Madge Gates Wallace
   D. Margaret Truman Daniel

10. HST's estate was approximately how much when he died in December 1972?
    A. Less than $100,000
    B. $225,000
    C. $600,000
    D. $1.425 million

11. To whom did HST leave the bulk of his estate?
    A. The Harry S. Truman Presidential Library
    B. Bess Truman
    C. Margaret Truman and her four sons
    D. Bess Truman and Margaret Truman

12. After Harry's death in 1972, what happened to the contents of the house?
    A. "Left as if the home had been frozen in time...."
    B. Inventoried and appraised by National Park Service
    C. Transferred to the Harry Truman Presidential Institute
    D. Assigned to the National Historic Trust

13. In October 1982, Bess's executors and Margaret did what with the residence?
    A. Deeded the residence to the people of the United States
    B. Donated the residence to the state of Missouri
    C. Transferred ownership to the Grand Masonic Lodge of Missouri
    D. Sold the residence to an undisclosed buyer

End of Life—*Answers*

1. A. "I don't know what history will say about me. But I can honestly say I did the best I could." (Sand, 1993, p. ix)
2. B. A fall in the bathroom which cracked a couple of ribs and cut his head (Hamby, 1995, pp. 633–634)
3. B. "It looks like a damn fine show...I just hate that I won't be around to see it." (Keyes, 1995, p. 121)
4. B. HST believed that a person's life should speak for itself. (Burnes, 2003, p. 232)
5. C. Bess Truman (Hamby, 1995, p. 634)
6. D. Auditorium, Truman Library (Hamby, 1995, p. 634)
7. B. Truman Beach (Wolz & Hayo, 2012, p. 152)
8. B. "I want to be out there so I can get up and walk into my office if I want to." (Burnes, 2003, p. 230)
9. C. Madge Gates Wallace (Caroli, 1989, p. 358)
10. C. $600,000 (Johnson, 1989, p. 129)
11. D. Bess Truman and Margaret Truman (Johnson, 1989, p. 129)
12. A. "Left as if the home had been frozen in time...." (Richardson, 2019)
13. A. Deeded the residence to the people of the United States (Taylor, 2013, pp. 120, 123)

Legacy

What is one legacy for which HST gets little credit?

1. What did Harry identify as "the greatest honor of his life"?
   A. Being Bess's husband, Margaret's father
   B. Winning the 1948 election
   C. Serving as Grand Master Mason of Missouri
   D. Commanding Battery D in World War I

2. HST denied that he had ever gave anyone "hell." He had done what?
   A. "I just tell the truth on them and they think it is hell!"
   B. "I just made the facts clear enough for a six-year-old to understand."
   C. "I can't think of anyone who deserves more hell than the Republican crowd."
   D. "'Hell' is in the mind of the guilty."

3. When President-elect Eisenhower visited Washington after winning the 1952 election, what did HST do?
   A. Insisted that he stay at the White House
   B. Met Ike at the train station
   C. Gave government workers time off to see Ike's motorcade
   D. Doubled Eisenhower's Secret Service protection

4. How did Boss Tom Pendergast describe HST?
   A. "The contrariest man [cuss] in Missouri."
   B. "The most honest politician in Missouri who cares about voters."
   C. "A politician who *could* have become very wealthy."
   D. "The straightest-shooting Baptist I have ever met."

5. One week before Oscar Collazo was to be executed for attempting to assassinate him, what action did HST take?

A. Ordered the courts to reexamine the trial

B. Commuted his sentence to life imprisonment

C. Suspended all executions in federal penitentiaries

D. Pardoned him

6. What is one legacy for which HST gets little credit?

A. Placed the White House under the National Park Service

B. Used his influence to institutionalize the ex-presidency

C. Lobbied for superdelegates to national political conventions

D. Instituted tax credits for large donors to presidential libraries

7. On what occasion did HST say, "We feel we have done our best in the public service. I hope and believe we have contributed to the welfare of this nation and to the peace of the world."?

A. Farewell Address to the American People, January 15, 1953

B. His last State of the Union

C. Final interview with *The New York Times*

D. A letter left on the Oval Office desk for Dwight Eisenhower

8. Given his workload, why did HST dislike being called "an elder statesman"?

A. "If the old pros sit on the sidelines, how will the next generation get the hang of politics?"

B. "I like being a nose buster and ass kicker much better."

C. "Every once in a while I still feel the need to stir things up a bit."

D. "I never, never want to be like some old politicians sitting around babbling about 'the good old days'!"

9. What HST innovation to the physical White House has been enjoyed by subsequent presidential families?
   A. Expanded the West Wing
   B. Moved the grand staircase to the entrance hall
   C. Built the Truman Balcony
   D. Added baths to the guest rooms

10. What were, according to the American Presidency Project, HST's poll numbers when he left the White House?
   A. 23% approval
   B. 31% approval
   C. 34% approval
   D. 37% approval

11. What were HST's approval numbers at rock bottom in November 1951?
   A. 19%
   B. 23%
   C. 35%
   D. 41%

12. How is HST currently ranked as a president, according to C-SPAN's 2017 poll of 91 presidential historians?
   A. 5th
   B. 6th
   C. 10th
   D. 18th

13. What was HST's major concern following Kennedy's assassination?
   A. The ability of Lyndon Johnson to step into Kennedy's shoes
   B. The impact on Caroline and John, Jr.
   C. Mrs. Kennedy's personal safety
   D. The degree of the CIA's involvement in the assassination

14. What did syndicated columnist Mary McGrory contend that HST proved during his years in the White House?
    A. "A president can be a human being"
    B. "The president doesn't have to be right all the time. Just most of the time."
    C. "The president does not have to be the smartest man in the room."
    D. "What Americans want from a president is the plain, unvarnished truth."

15. What presidential candidate, years later, hoping to win a tough campaign, compared himself to HST: "I've been a Truman man, and I guess I'm kind of a Truman character"?
    A. George McGovern in 1972
    B. Jimmy Carter in 1980
    C. Hubert Humphrey in 1968
    D. Al Gore in 2000

16. Appearing on a popular television program, *Person-to-Person*, how did HST say he "hoped" to be remembered?
    A. "As the man who prevented World War III"
    B. "As the people's president."
    C. "As a man who did his damnedest!"
    D. "As a man who recognized his responsibility to every American citizen"

17. In 1952 HST instituted what lasting legacy?
    A. That all major party candidates receive Secret Service protection
    B. That candidates' past income tax returns be sealed for 25 years
    C. That candidates' spouses be given a tour of the White House and presidential living quarters
    D. That major party candidates for president receive intelligence briefings from the CIA

18. What did HST say he wanted from history?
    A. "You may not have agreed with me—but you admitted that I told the truth, even when it was uncomfortable."
    B. "If I appear in a bad light...that's just too bad."
    C. "The conviction that my administration did the right things for the right reasons."
    D. "That I was the second hardest working man to ever live at 1600 Pennsylvania Avenue."

19. President Richard Nixon wanted to award the Congressional Medal of Honor on Truman's 87th birthday? Why did HST decline?
    A. "There are thousands of dead soldiers in Arlington more deserving of the medal than me!"
    B. "I have not done anything which should be the reason for any award, congressional or otherwise."
    C. "Nixon's just trying to ease his jaded conscience."
    D. "I am afraid that it would set a bad precedent!"

20. Who assessed Truman's presidency: "Right on all the big things, wrong on all the small ones"?
    A. House Speaker Sam Rayburn
    B. David McCullough, historian
    C. Lyndon B. Johnson
    D. Henry Kissinger

21. Who praised HST's relationship with staff, "He stood by us through thick and thin, always eager to attribute successes to us and to accept for himself the full responsibility for failure"?
    A. George C. Marshall
    B. Clark Clifford
    C. Dean Acheson
    D. Rose Conway

22. What president invoked HST's name 17 times in a commencement address at West Point?

A. Jimmy Carter

B. Lyndon B. Johnson

C. George W. Bush

D. Bill Clinton

23. What did HST say was "the most important decision of his presidency"?

A. Ending World War II without invading Japan

B. Going ahead with the meeting to create the United Nations

C. Waging the war in Korea

D. Not running again in 1952

Legacy—*Answers*

1. C. Serving as Grand Master Mason of Missouri (Roberts, 2012, p. 70)
2. A. "I just tell the truth on them and they think it is hell!" (Beschloss, 2000, p. 399)
3. C. Gave government employees time off to see Ike's motorcade (Gibbs & Duffy, 2012, p. 90)
4. A. "The contrariest man [cuss] in Missouri." (Truman, 1955, p. 141)
5. B. Commuted his sentence to life imprisonment (Hamby, 1995, p. 472)
6. B. Used his influence to institutionalize the ex-presidency. (Giglio, 1989, pp. 304–305)
7. A. Farewell Address to the American people, January 15, 1953 (Keyes, 2012, p. 166)
8. B. "I like being a nose buster and ass kicker much better." (McCullough, 1992, p. 969)
9. C. Built the Truman Balcony (Truman, 2004, p. 40; Hamby, 1995, p. 468)
10. B. 31% approval (McCoy, 1989, p. 287)
11. B. 23% (McCoy, 1989, p. 287)
12. B. 6th (Lamb & Swaim, 2019, p. 81)
13. D. The degree of the CIA's involvement in the assassination (Truman, December 22, 1963, p. all)
14. A. "A president can be a human being." (Ridings & McIver, 2000, p. 213)
15. C. Hubert Humphrey in 1968 (Schumacher, 2018, p. 392)
16. B. "As the people's president" (Sand, 1993, p. 39)
17. D. That major party candidates for president receive intelligence briefings from the CIA (Clapper & Brown, 2018, p. 345)
18. B. "If I appear in a bad light...that's just too bad." (Walsh, 2005, p. 211)

19. B. "I have not done anything which should be the reason for any award, congressional or otherwise." (Robbins, 1980, p. 184)
20. A. House Speaker Sam Rayburn (Ferrell, 1983, p. 167)
21. C. Dean Acheson (Robbins, 1979, p. 152)
22. C. George W. Bush (Algeo, 2009, p. 230)
23. C. Waging the war in Korea (Beschloss, 2018, p. 486)

Conclusion

So how did you do? What questions stumped you or left you scratching your head? What questions left you saying, "Never heard about *that* in my American history classes." As a boy in Independence, Missouri, Harry Truman discovered that history has extremely valuable lessons to transmit. Consequently, he argued, "There is nothing new in the world except the history you do not know" (Keyes, 1995, p. 39). And, I would add, the *biography* you should know.

Harry Truman was a remarkable leader; a leader who knew how to lead! A leader who led without consulting the polls. A leader who believed in doing "the right thing" rather than the politically expedient thing. A leader who conceded there were "probably hundreds of people" "better qualified than I am to be president. But they weren't elected" (Keyes, 1995, p. 61). I can only begin to imagine what he would say about the current practice of political leadership at the local, state, and federal levels.

What I know is that between April 12, 1945 and January 20, 1953, he did his best. He once said, "I have tried my best to give the nation everything I had in me" (Keyes). Harry Truman was taken by an epitaph he observed on a gravestone in Tombstone, Arizona: "Here lies Jack Williams. He done his damndest." Truman explained, "that is the greatest epitaph that a man can have" (Keyes).

Sources for *Almost Everything Worth Knowing About Harry S Truman*

Algeo, M. (2009). *Harry Truman's excellent adventure: The true story of a great American road trip.* Chicago, IL: Chicago Review Press.

Allen, E. W. (1989). Public opinion polling. In R. S. Kirkendall, (Ed.). *The Harry S. Truman encyclopedia* (pp. 290–291). Boston, MA: G. K. Hall.

Ambrose, S. E. (1989). Eisenhower, Dwight David. In R. S. Kirkendall, (Ed.). *The Harry S. Truman encyclopedia* (pp. 108–109). Boston, MA: G. K. Hall.

Angelo, B. (2005). *First families: The impact of the White House on their lives.* New York, NY: William Morrow.

Anthony, C. (2012, June 28). Reagan campaigns for Truman. Retrieved from https://carlanthonyonline.com/2012/06/28/reagan-campaigns-for-truman

Anthony, C. (2013, September 4). Bess Truman rocks the back porch & her only recorded interview. Retrieved from https://carlanthonyonline.com/2013/09/ 04/bess-truman-rocks-the-back-home-porch-her-only-recorded-interview

Baime, A. J. (2017). *The accidental President: Harry S. Truman and the four months that changed the world.* New York, NY: Houghton Mifflin.

Barnes, C. A. (2006). Vinson, Fred(erick) M(oore). In T. S. Uebelhor, (Ed.). *Presidential profiles: The Truman years* (pp. 616–618). New York, NY: Facts on File.

Baughman, J .L. (2006). McCarthy, Joseph Raymond. In T. S. Uebelhor, (Ed.). *Presidential profiles: The Truman years* (pp. 351–357). New York, NY: Facts on File.

Beschloss, M. (1997). *Taking charge: The Johnson White House tapes, 1963–1964.* New York, NY: Touchstone.

Beschloss, M. (Ed.). (2000). *American Heritage illustrated history of the presidents.* New York, NY: Crown.

Beschloss, M. (2007). *Presidential courage: Brave leaders and how they changed America, 1789–1989.* New York, NY: Simon & Schuster.

Beschloss, M. (2014, May 8). Harry Truman's formidable mother-in-law. *The New York Times*, np.

Beschloss, M. (2015, February 28). L.B.J. and Truman: The bond that helped forge Medicare. *The New York Times*, np.

Beschloss, M. (2018). *Presidents of war: The epic story from 1807 to modern times.* New York, NY: Crown.

Best, G. D. (1989). Hoover, Herbert Clark. In R. S. Kirkendall, (Ed.). *The Harry S. Truman encyclopedia* (pp. 157–159). Boston, MA: G. K. Hall.

Bickerton, I. J. (1989). Jacobson, Eddie. In R. S. Kirkendall, (Ed.). *The Harry S. Truman encyclopedia* (pp. 185–186). Boston, MA: G. K. Hall.

Bolt, R. (1992, October). President Harry S. Truman: Independent Baptist from Independence. *Missouri Historical Review, 87*(1), 36–47.

Brands, H. W. (2010). *American dreams: The United States since 1945.* New York, NY: Penguin Press.

Brandus, P. (2015). *Under this roof: The White House and the presidency.* Guilford, CT: Lyons Press.

Breitman, R., & Lichtman, A. J. (2013). *FDR and the Jews.* Cambridge, MA: Belknap Press of Harvard University Press.

Brower, K. A. (2016). *First women: The grace and power of America's modern ladies.* New York, NY: Harper.

Brower, K. A. (2018). *First in line: Presidents, vice presidents, and the pursuit of power.* New York, NY: Harper.

Burnes, B., & Martin, D. (2003). *Harry S. Truman: His life and times.* Kansas City, MO: Kansas City Star Books.

Caroli, B. B. (1989). Truman, Elizabeth Virginia Wallace ("Bess"). In R. S. Kirkendall, (Ed.). *The Harry S. Truman encyclopedia* (pp. 357–359). Boston, MA: G. K. Hall.

Caroli, B. B. (1995). *First ladies.* (Expanded edition). New York, NY: Oxford University Press.

Champagne, A. (1989). Rayburn, Sam. In R. S. Kirkendall, (Ed.). *The Harry S. Truman encyclopedia* (pp. 294–295). Boston, MA: G. K. Hall.

Clapper, J. R., & Brown, T. (2018). *Facts and fears: Hard truths from a life in intelligence.* New York, NY: Viking.

Curtis, G. H. (1989). Reading. In R. S. Kirkendall, (Ed.). *The Harry S. Truman encyclopedia* (pp. 295–296). Boston, MA: G. K. Hall.

Dallek, R. (2008). *Harry S. Truman: The thirty-third president.* New York, NY: Henry Holt Times Books.

Daniels, C. T. (2017, September 20). Personal Interview. Harry S. Truman Presidential Library, Independence, MO.

Doenecke, J. D. (1989). China. In R. S. Kirkendall, (Ed.), *The Harry S. Truman encyclopedia* (pp. 48–51). Boston, MA: G. K. Hall.

Donovan, R. J. (1982). *Tumultuous years: The presidency of Harry S. Truman, 1949–1953.* New York, NY: W. W. Norton.

Dorough, C. D. (1962). *Mr. Sam: A biography of Samuel T. Rayburn, speaker of the house.* New York, NY: Random House.

Dorsett, L. (1996). Truman and the Pendergast machine. *MidContinental American Studies Journal, 7*(2), 1–27.

Doss, Desmond biography. http://www.findagrave.com/memorial/13711681/desmond-thomas-doss

Dunar, A. J. (1989). Battery D. In R. S. Kirkendall, (Ed.). *The Harry S. Truman encyclopedia* (pp. 357–359). Boston, MA: G. K. Hall.

Dunar, A. J. (1989). Military career. In R. S. Kirkendall, (Ed.). *The Harry S. Truman encyclopedia* (pp. 235–236). Boston, MA: G. K. Hall.

Eisenhower, D. D. (1963). *The White House Years: Mandate for change: 1953–1956: A personal account*. New York, NY: Doubleday.

Elliott, D. A. (1989). Wherry, Kenneth Spicer. In T. S. Uebelhor, (Ed.). *Presidential profiles: The Truman years* (p. 635). New York, NY: Facts on File.

Ellis, R. J. (2008). *Presidential travel: The journey from George Washington to George W. Bush*. Lawrence: University Press of Kansas.

Failing health at age 80 forced slowdown in habits. (1972, December 26). *The Oakland Tribune*, p. 5.

Ferrell, R. H. (Ed.). (1980/2002). *The autobiography of Harry S. Truman*. Columbia: University of Missouri Press.

Ferrell, R. H. (Ed.). (1980). *Off the record: The private papers of Harry S. Truman*. Columbia: The University of Missouri Press.

Ferrell, R. H. (1983). *Harry S. Truman and the modern American presidency*. Boston, MA: Little, Brown & Company.

Ferrell, R. H. (Ed.). (1991). *Truman in the White House: The diary of Eben A. Ayers*. Columbia: University of Missouri Press.

Ferrell, R. H. (1996). *Harry S. Truman: A life*. Columbia: University of Missouri Press.

Figman, E. (2006). Thomas, J(ohn) Parnell. In T. S. Uebelhor, (Ed.). *Presidential profiles: The Truman years* (pp. 574–576). New York, NY: Facts on File.

Flanders, J. (2006). Marshall, Thurgood. In T. S. Uebelhor, (Ed.). *Presidential profiles: The Truman years* (pp. 387–388). New York, NY: Facts on File.

Frank, J. (2013). *Ike and Dick: Portrait of a strange political marriage.* New York, NY: Simon & Schuster.

Fromkin, D. (1995). *In the time of the Americans: FDR, Truman, Eisenhower, Marshall, MacArthur—The generation that changed America's role in the world.* New York, NY: Alfred A. Knopf.

Gardiner, M. R. (2002). *Harry Truman and civil rights: Moral courage and political risks.* Carbondale: Southern Illinois University Press.

Gergel, R. (2019). *Unexamined courage: The blinding of Sgt. Isaac Woodard and the awakening of President Harry S. Truman and Judge J. Waties Waring.* New York, NY: Sarah Crichton Books.

Geselbracht, R. H. (2001, Spring). Mutual admiration and a few jokes: The correspondence of Harry Truman with Groucho and Harpo Marx. *Prologue, 33*(1), 45–50.

Geselbracht, R. H. (Ed.). (2007). *The civil rights legacy of Harry S. Truman.* Kirksville, MO: Truman State University Press.

Giangreco, D. M., & Moore, K. (1999). *Dear Harry: Truman's mailroom, 1945–1953.* Mechanicsburg, PA: Stackpole.

Gibbs, N., & Duffy, M. (2012). *The president's club: Inside the world's most exclusive fraternity.* New York, NY: Simon & Schuster.

Giglio, J. N. (1989). Retirement. In R. S. Kirkendall, (Ed.). *The Harry S. Truman encyclopedia* (pp. 304–305). Boston, MA: G. K. Hall.

Grinder, D., & Shaw, S. (2011). *The presidents and their faith: From George Washington to Barack Obama.* Boise, ID: Russell Media Web.

Hamby, A. L. (1995). *Man of the people: A life of Harry S. Truman.* New York, NY: Oxford University Press.

Hamilton, N. (2010). *American Caesars: From Franklin D.*

Roosevelt to George W. Bush. New Haven, CT: Yale University Press.

Harrison, T. L. (2006). Lewis, John L[lewellyn]. In T. S. Uebelhor, (Ed.). *Presidential profiles: The Truman years* (pp. 322–325). New York, NY: Facts on File.

Healy, P. (2015, October 31). Assassination attempt on President Truman fails. *The New York Daily News*.

Heath, J. E. (1989). Truman Committee. In R. S. Kirkendall, (Ed.). *The Harry S. Truman encyclopedia* (p. 364). Boston, MA: G. K. Hall.

Hedley, J. H. (1979). *Harry S. Truman: The 'little' man from Missouri: A revealing account of the man and the momentous decisions he made*. Woodbury, NY: Barron's.

Heller, F.H. (1989). Truman, John Anderson. In R. S. Kirkendall, (Ed.). *The Harry S. Truman encyclopedia* (pp. 359–360). Boston, MA: G. K. Hall.

Hershey, J. (1946, August 31). Hiroshima. *The New Yorker*, 15–26.

Hillman, W. (1984). *Harry S. Truman in his own words: A collection*. New York, NY: Bonanza Books.

Hillstrom, K. (2011). *Defining moments: McCarthyism and the communist threat*. Detroit, MI: Omnigraphics.

History.com. (Eds.). (2019, June 7). This day in history, July 25, 1945: Truman drops hint to Stalin about a terrible new weapon. Retrieved from https://www.histo ry.com/this-day-in-history/truman-drops-hint-to -stalin-about-a-terrible-new-weapon

Hoff-Wilson, J. (1989). Nixon, Richard M. In R. S. Kirkendall, (Ed.). *The Harry S. Truman encyclopedia* (pp. 125–126). Boston, MA: G. K. Hall.

Holmes, D. L. (2012). *Faiths of the postwar presidents: From Truman to Obama*. Athens: The University of Georgia Press.

Independence Productions. (1964). *Decisions: The conflicts of Harry S. Truman*, episode 6, "At war with the experts. Film Collection. Harry S. Truman Presidential Library, Independence, MO.

Israel, F. L. (Ed.). (2003). *The education of the presidents of the United States*. Philadelphia, PA: Mason Crest.

It's an all-day and nearly all-night job. (1952, February 24). *The New York Times*, p.1E.

Jeansonne, G. (2016). *Herbert Hoover: A life*. New York, NY: New American Library.

Jenks, P. E. (n.d.). Mr. Truman and the Baptists. *American Baptist*, Vertical File, Harry S. Truman Presidential Library, Independence, MO.

Johnson, N. M. (1989). Finances, personal. In R. S. Kirkendall, (Ed.). *The Harry S. Truman encyclopedia* (p. 129). Boston, MA: G. K. Hall.

Johnson, N. M. (1999). *Power, money, and women: Words to the wise from Harry S. Truman*. Independence, MO: Niel M. Johnson.

Kane, J. N., & Podell, J. (2009). *Facts about the presidents: A compilation of biographical and historical information* (8th ed.). New York, NY: H. W. Wilson.

Kaplan, L. S. (1989). North Atlantic Treaty Organization. In R. S. Kirkendall, (Ed.). *The Harry S. Truman encyclopedia* (pp. 258–260). Boston, MA: G. K. Hall.

Keyes, R. (2012). *The wit and wisdom of Harry Truman: A treasury of quotations, anecdotes, and observations* (2nd ed.). Boston, MA: David Scott Publisher.

Kirk, E. K. (1986). *Music at the White House: A history of the American spirit*. Urbana: University of Illinois Press.

Kirkendall, R. S. (Ed.). (1989). *The Harry S. Truman encyclopedia*. Boston, MA: G. K. Hall.

Kirkendall, R. S. (1989). Wallace, Henry Agard. In R. S. Kirkendall, (Ed.). *The Harry S. Truman encyclopedia* (pp. 383–385). Boston, MA: G. K. Hall.

Kirkendall, R. S. (2008). Faith and foreign policy: An exploration into the mind of Harry Truman. *Missouri Historical Review, 102*(4), 214–224.

Klara, R. (2010). *FDR's funeral train: A betrayed widow, a Soviet spy, and a presidency in the balance.* New York, NY: Palgrave Macmillan.

Klara, R. (2013). *The hidden White House: Harry Truman and the reconstruction of America's most famous residence.* New York, NY: Thomas Dunne/St. Martin's Press.

Knott, S. F. (2019). The lost soul of the American presidency: The decline into demagoguery and the prospects for renewal. Lawrence: University Press of Kansas.

Knutson, L. L. (2014). *Away from the White House: Presidential escapes, retreats, and vacations.* Washington, DC: White House Historical Association.

Knutson, L. L. (2006). Truman Beach: The 33rd president at Key West. *White House History, 18,* 400–415.

Koterba, E. V. (1960, September 2). Truman bounces in and out. *The Pittsburgh Press,* p. 18.

Kundhardt, P. B., Jr., Kundhardt, P. B., III, & Kundhardt, P. W. (1999). *The American president.* New York, NY: Riverhead.

Lamb, B., & Swain. S. (2019). *The presidents: Noted historians rank American's best—and worst—chief executives.* New York, NY: PublicAffairs.

Leffler, M. P. (1992). *A preponderance of power: National security, the Truman administration, and the Cold War.* Palo Alto, CA: Stanford University Press.

Leonard, T. M. (2006). MacArthur, Douglas. In T. S. Uebelhor, (Ed.). *Presidential profiles: The Truman years* (pp. 345–347). New York, NY: Facts on File.

Lepore, J. (2018). *These truths: A history of the United States.* New York, NY: W. W. Norton.

Leuchtenburg, W. E. (2005*). The White House looks south: Franklin D. Roosevelt, Harry S. Truman, and Lyndon B. Johnson.* Baton Rouge, LA: LSU Press.

Leuchtenburg, W. E. (2015). *The American president: From*

Teddy Roosevelt to Bill Clinton. New York, NY: Oxford University Press.

Loewenheim, F. L. (1989). Press, The. In R. S. Kirkendall, (Ed.). *The Harry S. Truman encyclopedia* (pp. 287–289). Boston, MA: G. K. Hall.

Mancini, M. (2016, March 1). Who were the president's favorite presidents? *Mental Floss.* Retrieved from http://mentalfloss.com/article/59186/favorite-us-presidents-8-us-presidents

Matuz, R. (2004). *The presidents' fact book: A comprehensive handbook.* New York, NY: Black Dog & Leventhal.

McCoy, D. R. (1989). Presidency. In R. S. Kirkendall, (Ed.). *The Harry S. Truman encyclopedia* (pp. 285–287). Boston, MA: G. K. Hall.

McCullough, D. (1986). The unexpected Harry Truman. In W. Zinsser (Ed.), *Extraordinary lives: The art and craft of American biography* (pp. 23–61). New York, NY: American Heritage.

McCullough, D. (1992). *Truman.* New York, NY: Simon & Schuster.

Melton, D. (1980). *Harry S. Truman: The man who walked with giants.* Independence, MO: Independence Press.

Merkley, P. C. (2004). *American presidents, religion, and Israel: The heirs of Cyrus.* Westport, CT: Praeger.

Merkley, P. C. (2008). "I am Cyrus." *Christian History & Biography, 99,* 30–32. Retrieved from https://christianhistory institute.org/magazine/article/i-am-cyrus

Miller, W. L. (2012). *Two Americans: Truman, Eisenhower, and a dangerous world.* New York, NY: Knopf.

Miller, M. (1973). *Plain speaking: An oral biography of Harry S. Truman.* New York, NY: Berkley.

Morris, S. J. (2014). *Price of fame: The honorable Clare Booth Luce.* New York, NY: Random House.

Murphy, P. L. (1989). Vinson, Frederick M. In R. S. Kirkendall, (Ed.). *The Harry S. Truman encyclopedia* (pp. 380–381). Boston, MA: G. K. Hall.

Neal, S. (2001). *Harry and Ike: The partnership that remade the postwar world*. New York, NY: Touchstone.

Neiberg, M. (2016). *Potsdam: The end of World War II and the remaking of Europe*. New York, NY: Basic Books.

Parmet, H. S. (1989). Kennedy, John F. In R. S. Kirkendall, (Ed.). *The Harry S. Truman encyclopedia* (pp.197–198). Boston, MA: G. K. Hall.

Pemberton, W. E. (1989). Farm experience. In R. S. Kirkendall, (Ed.). *The Harry S. Truman encyclopedia* (pp.125–126). Boston, MA: G. K. Hall.

Pemberton, W. E. (1989). *Harry S. Truman: Fair dealer and cold warrior*. Boston, MA: Twayne.

Pemberton, W. E. (1989). Jackson County Court. In R. S. Kirkendall, (Ed.). *The Harry S. Truman encyclopedia* (pp. 184–185). Boston, MA: G. K. Hall.

Peraino, K. (2017). *A force so swift: Mao, Truman, and the birth of modern China, 1949*. New York, NY: Crown.

Peretti, B. W. (2012). *The leading man: Hollywood and the presidential image*. New Brunswick, NJ: Rutgers University Press.

Peters, G., & Woolley, J. T. (1972, December 26). *Richard Nixon: Statement on the Death of Harry S Truman*. The American Presidency Project. Retrieved from http://www. presidency.ucsb.edu/ws/?pid=372

Rasmussen, R. K. (2005). *The fifties in America* (Vol. 3): *Jackie Robinson—youth culture and the generation gap*. Pasadena, CA: Salem Press

Reid, D. (2016). *The brazen age: New York City and the American empire: Politics, art, and bohemia*. New York, NY: Pantheon Books.

Richardson, D. J. email, July 5, 2019.

Ridings, W. J., and Molver, S. B. (2000). *Rating the presidents: A ranking of U.S. leaders, from the great and honorable to the dishonest and incompetent*. New York, NY: Citadel.

Riley, G. (1989). Truman, Mary Jane. In R. S. Kirkendall, (Ed.). *The Harry S. Truman encyclopedia* (p. 362). Boston, MA: G. K. Hall.

Robbins, C., & Smith, B. (1979). *Last of his kind: An informal portrait of Harry S. Truman.* New York, NY: William Morrow.

Robbins, J. (1980). *Harry & Bess: An American love story.* New York, NY: G. P. Putnam.

Roberts, A. E. (2012). *Brother Truman: The Masonic life and philosophy of Harry S. Truman.* Aylett, VA: Anchor Communications.

Rockwell, S. W. (1976, July 8). Oral history. Harry S. Truman Presidential Library, Independence, MO.

Rose, L. A. (1999). *The Cold War comes to Main Street: America in 1950.* Lawrence: University Press of Kansas.

Sand, G. W. (1993). *Truman in retirement: A former president views the nation & the world.* South Bend, IN: Justice Books.

Schneider, S. R. (2013, October 23). The neckties of President Harry S. Truman. *Gentlemen's Gazette,* https://www.gentlemansgazette.com/ties-neckties-harry-truman

Schumacher, M. (2018). *The contest: The 1968 election and the war for America's soul.* Minneapolis: University of Minnesota.

Schweikart, L., & Lynch, D. (1994). Government and politics. In R. Layman, (Ed.), *American decades 1950–1959.* (pp. 179–234). Detroit, MI: Gale Research.

Seale, W. (2008). *The president's house.* White House Historical Association, Washington, DC.

Seeley, M. E. (1996). *Season's greetings from the White House: The collection of presidential Christmas cards, messages and gifts.* New York, NY: MasterMedia.

Sides, H. (2018). *On desperate ground: The marines at the reservoir: The Korean War's greatest battle.* New York, NY: Doubleday.

Skidmore, M. J. (2004). *After the White House: Former presidents as private citizens.* New York, NY: Palgrave Macmillan.

Spann, C. E., & Williams, M. E., Sr. (2008). *Presidential praise: Our presidents and their hymns.* Macon, GA: Mercer University Press.

Spitz, B. (2018). *Reagan: An American journey.* New York, NY: Penguin.

Steil, B. (2018). *The Marshall Plan: Dawn of the Cold War.* New York, NY: Simon & Schuster.

Sullivan, A. M. (2004). Harry S. Truman. In F. L. Israel, (Ed.), *Taught to lead: The education of the presidents of the United States* (pp. 350–359). Philadelphia, PA: Mason Crest.

Summers, A. (2000). *The arrogance of power: The secret world of Richard Nixon.* New York, NY: Viking.

Taylor, J. E. (2013). *Harry Truman's Independence: The center of the world.* Charleston, SC: History Press.

Theoharis, A. (1989). Hoover, John Edgar. In R. S. Kirkendall, (Ed.). *The Harry S. Truman encyclopedia* (pp. 159–161). Boston, MA: G. K. Hall.

Timberlake, C. E. (1989). Stalin, Joseph. In R. S. Kirkendall, (Ed.). *The Harry S. Truman encyclopedia* (pp. 338–339). Boston, MA: G. K. Hall.

Tracy, S. J. (2006). Smith, Margaret Chase. In T. S. Uebelhor, (Ed.). *Presidential profiles: The Truman years* (pp. 530–532). New York, NY: Facts on File.

Troy, G. (1989). Assassination attempt. In R. S. Kirkendall, (Ed.). *The Harry S. Truman encyclopedia* (p. 13). Boston, MA: G. K. Hall.

Truman at Potsdam. (June/July 1980). In *American Heritage, 31*(4) Retrieved from https://www.americanheritage.com/content/truman-potsdam

Truman, H. S. (1947, June 28). Reinforcing the commitment of the federal government to guaranteeing civil rights for all citizens and combating discrimination. Fourth draft, speech to NAACP, with corrections by Harry S. Truman. Papers of Harry S. Truman: President's Secretary's File. Harry S. Truman Presidential Library, Independence, MO.

Truman, H. S. (1948, September 21). Address at the Mormon Tabernacle, Salt Lake City, UT. Harry S. Truman Presidential Library, Independence, MO.

Truman, H. S. (1952, January 3). Comments on Weight and Clothes. Diary Entry by Harry Truman. Harry S. Truman Presidential Library, Independence, MO.

Truman, H. S. (1952, October 17). Speech for the Conference of the National Jewish Welfare Board, Jewish Virtual Library, http://jewishvirtuallibrary.org

Truman, H. S. (1966). *Personal papers of Harry S. Truman: 1952–1953*. Harry S. Truman Presidential Library, Independence, MO.

Truman, H. S. (1953, January 15). The President's farewell address to the American public. HST Papers, 1945–1953, Provided courtesy of The American Presidency Project. John Woolley and Gerhard Peters. University of California, Santa Barbara.

Truman, H. S. (1953, November) *Harry Truman on McCarthyism*, CBS Radio, Retrieved from https://www.youtube.com/watch?v=Yg_lpco009A

Truman, H. S. (1953). *Mr. Citizen*. New York, NY: Bernard Geis Associates.

Truman, H. S. (1955). *Memoirs, vol. 1: Year of trial and hope*. Garden City, NY: Doubleday.

Truman, H. S. (1956). *Memoirs, vol. 2: Year of Decisions*. Garden City, NY: Doubleday.

Truman is asked to prove charge. (1960, April 20). *The New York Times*.

Truman, H. S. to D. Acheson. (1960, October 9). Richard Nixon. Truman Papers (PPF File, Box 1). Harry S. Truman Presidential Library, Independence, MO.

Truman, H. S. (1963, December 22). Limit CIA's role to intelligence. *The Washington Post*, p. A-3.

Truman, M. (1973). *Harry S. Truman*. New York, NY: William Morrow.

Truman, M. (1989). *Where the buck stops: The personal and private writings of Harry S. Truman*. New York, NY: Grand Central.

Truman, M. (2004). *The president's house: 1800 to the present: Secrets and history of the world's most famous home*. New York, NY: Ballantine Books.

Truman-Nixon chill. (1986, February 23). *The New York Times*. Archives. Harry S. Truman Presidential Library, Independence, MO.

Truman Places, (n.d.) First Baptist Church of Grandview. Harry S. Truman Presidential Library, Independence, MO.

Uebelhor, T. S. (2006). Marshall, George Catlett. In T. S. Uebelhor, (Ed.). *Presidential profiles: The Truman years* (pp. 379–389). New York, NY: Facts on File.

Uebelhor, T. S. (2006). Truman, Elizabeth Virginia Wallace. In T. S. Uebelhor, (Ed.). *Presidential profiles: The Truman years* (pp. 585–586). New York, NY: Facts on File.

Uebelhor, T. S. (2006). Truman, Harry S. In T. S. Uebelhor, (Ed.). *Presidential profiles: The Truman years* (pp. 586–597). New York, NY: Facts on File.

Wacker, G. (2009). Billy Graham's America. *Church History*, *78*(3), 489–511.

Walker, J. S. (1997). *Prompt & utter destruction: Truman and the use of atomic bombs against Japan*. Chapel Hill: University of North Carolina Press.

Wallace, P. W. (1995). *Politics of conscience: A biography of Margaret Chase Smith*. Westport, CT: Praeger.

Walsh, K. T. (2005). *From Mount Vernon to Crawford: A history of the presidents and their retreats*. New York, NY: Hyperion.

Weisbrode, K. (2016). *The year of indecision, 1946: A tour through the crucible of Harry Truman's America.* New York, NY: Viking.

White, P. (2014). *Whistle stop: How 31,000 miles of train travel, 352 speeches and a little Midwest gumption saved the presidency of Harry Truman.* Lebanon, NH: ForeEdge/ University Press of New England.

Whitman, A. (1972, December 27). Harry S. Truman: Decisive president. *The New York Times.* p. 46.

Williams, B. (2005, August 6). *President Truman on his decision to drop the atomic bomb.* NBC Learn, NBC Nightly News. Retrieved from https://archives. nbclearn .com/portal/site/k-12/browse?cue card=4962

Witcover, J. (2014). *The American vice-presidency: From irrelevance to power.* New York, NY: Smithsonian.

Withers, B. (1996). *The president travels by train: Politics and Pullmans.* Lynchburg, VA: TLC Publishing.

Wolz & Hayo. (2012). *Presidents in Paradise: The legacy of the Harry S. Truman Little White House.* Key West, FL: Historic Tours of America.

Wyden, P. H. (1985). *Day one: Before Hiroshima and after.* New York, NY: Simon & Schuster.

Yates, L. A. (1989). Fair Deal. In R. S. Kirkendall, (Ed.). *The Harry S. Truman encyclopedia* (pp. 123–125). Boston, MA: G. K. Hall.

Yates, L. A. (1989). Key West. In R. S. Kirkendall, (Ed.). *The Harry S. Truman encyclopedia* (p. 200). Boston, MA: G. K. Hall.

Yates, L. A. (1989). Religion. In R. S. Kirkendall, (Ed.). *The Harry S. Truman encyclopedia* (p. 303). Boston, MA: G. K. Hall.

Yates, L. A. (1989). *Williamsburg,* USS. In R. S. Kirkendall, (Ed.). *The Harry S. Truman encyclopedia* (p. 388). Boston, MA: G. K. Hall.

Zangrando, R. L. (1989). National Association for the Advancement of Colored People. In R. S. Kirkendall,

(Ed.). *The Harry S. Truman encyclopedia* (p. 250). Boston, MA: G. K. Hall.

Zinsser, W. (Ed.). (1986). *Extraordinary lives: The art and craft of American biography* (pp. 23–61). New York, NY: American Heritage.

Zobrist, B. K. (1989). Independence, Missouri. In R. S. Kirkendall, (Ed.). *The Harry S. Truman encyclopedia* (pp. 170–171). Boston, MA: G. K. Hall.

About the Author

Harold Ivan Smith has spent more than a decade researching *Almost Everything Worth Knowing About Harry S Truman: 33rd President of the United States*, who entered the Oval Office following the unexpected death of Franklin D. Roosevelt. Smith has a doctorate from Asbury Theological Seminary and an EdS from Peabody College of Vanderbilt University. He is a member of the Wild About Harry Society of the Truman Library Institute in Kansas City, Missouri. He has lectured at the Roosevelt Reading Festival at the Franklin D. Roosevelt Presidential Library and at the Harry S. Truman Presidential Library. His research, conducted in 10 presidential libraries, focuses on the bereavements of U.S. presidents and first ladies. *Eleanor: A Spiritual Biography*, his most recent book, examines how Eleanor Roosevelt's spirituality influenced her social and political activism. Smith, known as a storyteller, lives in Palm Springs, CA, and teaches "Grief at 1600 Pennsylvania Avenue" at the Learning in Retirement program at the College of the Desert.

Made in the USA
Monee, IL
18 April 2020